Eisen and Engler have provided parents of socially vulnerable children a wonderful resource. They skillfully discuss the various reasons children may be anxious in social settings and what parents can do about it. This book will help parents, mental health professionals, and others who work with youth sensitively assist those children who have much to offer but are standing by on the sidelines of life.

> —Mary A. Fristad, Ph.D, ABPP, professor of psychiatry and psychology at the Ohio State University and director of research and psychological services in the Division of Child and Adolescent Psychiatry

Eisen and Engler have authored a truly valuable work. Social problems in children are often complex, misunderstood, frustrating, and difficult for parents. Helping Your Socially Vulnerable Child *provides a reasoned and reasonable guide to understanding and helping children with social problems. These authors speak from science and experience. Their case-study approach provides an exceptional framework to assist parents in seeing the world through the eyes of their struggling children and providing much needed guidance and support. I will recommend this book without reservation to all of the families I work with.*

> —Sam Goldstein, Ph.D., professor of psychology at George Mason University and coauthor of *Raising a Self-Disciplined Child*

The book is filled with practical, easy-to-understand strategies that parents can use to help their socially vulnerable children fit in better with their peers. If your child is shy, withdrawn, impulsive, easily frustrated, or difficult to get along with, you should read this book!

> —Martin M. Antony, Ph.D., ABPP, professor of psychology at Ryerson University and Author of *The Shyness and Social Anxiety Workbook*

Edward Decy maintains that "the need to feel that you belong and are connected" is the first among the needs that are most motivating to a child. The development of social competence is as much an educational responsibility as is the development of academic skill. Unfortunately, this responsibility is often overlooked because social skill is expected to develop incidentally to being involved in the process of going to school. Where the system falls down, Eisen and Engler use their experience, empathy, and insight to give parents the means to stand up to the challenge of the socially vulnerable child. Helping Your Socially Vulnerable Child *provides parents the objectivity to recognize when a problems exists and the tools to fix it.*

> —G. Emerson Dickman, III, attorney specializing in the representation of children with disabilities and president of the board of directors of the International Dyslexia Association

Helping Your Socially Vulnerable Child

What to Do When Your
Child Is Shy, Socially
Anxious, Withdrawn,
or Bullied

ANDREW R. EISEN, PH.D.
LINDA B. ENGLER, PH.D.

New Harbinger Publications, Inc.

Publisher's Note

This publication is designed to provide accurate and authoritative information in regard to the subject matter covered. It is sold with the understanding that the publisher is not engaged in rendering psychological, financial, legal, or other professional services. If expert assistance or counseling is needed, the services of a competent professional should be sought.

Distributed in Canada by Raincoast Books

Copyright © 2007 by Andrew R. Eisen and Linda B. Engler
New Harbinger Publications, Inc.
5674 Shattuck Avenue
Oakland, CA 94609
www.newharbinger.com

Acquired by Catharine Sutker; Cover design by Amy Shoup;
Edited by Karen O'Donnell Stein; Text design by Tracy Carlson

Library of Congress Cataloging-in-Publication Data

Eisen, Andrew R.
  Helping your socially vulnerable child : what to do when your child is shy, socially anxious, withdrawn, or bullied / Andrew R. Eisen and Linda B. Engler.
      p. cm.
  ISBN 978-1-57224-458-0
  1. Bashfulness in children. 2. Anxiety in children. 3. Bullying. 4. Child rearing.
I. Engler, Linda B. II. Title.
  BF723.B3E57 2007
  649'.1567--dc22

                                                          2007007904

09 08 07

10 9 8 7 6 5 4 3 2 1

First printing

To our children, Zachary and Carly:
May you always retain your spirit and zest for life

In loving memory of Beatrice Block:
Always a source of inspiration and strength

To the parents of the children we've worked with:
For your unwavering dedication and commitment

Contents

Acknowledgments

As always, our heartfelt thanks to Cal and Phyllis Engler for being the charter members of our fan club. This book could not have been possible without their unceasing love, guidance, and support. We thank Catharine Sutker, our acquisitions editor at New Harbinger Publications, for embracing our concept of social vulnerability and for helping us shape our vision. Finally, special thanks to Karen O'Donnell Stein, our editor, for her careful attention to detail and most insightful comments and suggestions.

Introduction

As specialists in anxiety and related disorders, we are most often consulted by parents for our expertise in helping children and their families with separation anxiety, panic attacks, shyness, social fears, or obsessive-compulsive disorder (OCD). However, it has become increasingly evident to us that these children's struggles are not limited to anxiety. As we dig deeper, we often find that anxious youth struggle with other problems, such as impulsivity, distractibility, inflexibility, negativity, or explosive outbursts. What many of these children have in common is that they are *socially vulnerable*—they are prone to being neglected or actively rejected by their peers. *Helping Your Socially Vulnerable Child* is designed to help parents of these children, who may be experiencing shyness, mild to moderate social anxiety, social withdrawal, or social vulnerability.

Why This Book?

Many parenting books focus either on a single disorder, such as attention-deficit/hyperactivity disorder (ADHD) or OCD, or on several disorders, with specific chapters devoted to each disorder, providing readers with a great breadth of information. However, most children don't fit neatly into one category or another. Instead, they may have features of more than one disorder. Our book will help you understand how these different characteristics come together to affect your child's social functioning.

Helping Your Socially Vulnerable Child presents you with ten real-life stories, drawn from our extensive clinical experience. These are composite sketches of typical families we see in our practices. Of course, any distinguishing information has been disguised to protect the privacy of the families being depicted.

This novel approach will allow you to follow these families as they identify the types of social anxiety, withdrawal, and vulnerability experienced by their children and as they learn to recognize how multiple influences (for instance, temperament, sensitivity to anxiety, and neurological conditions) can interact with each other and impede their child's social adjustment. Finally, we will tag along with these families as they learn how to teach their children the coping strategies and social skills that will lead to better outcomes.

Now let's look at some factors that may interact with anxiety to create roadblocks for your child's social success. For instance, does your child regularly do any of the following?

- Misperceive others' intentions

- Misinterpret others' remarks

- Believe that nothing is ever his or her fault

- Explode without notice

- Complain of constant fatigue

- Insist on doing everything his or her way

If any of the above behaviors are familiar to you, you know that they can disrupt the quality of your family life. Parents are often able to forgive and forget these behaviors. Your child's peers, teachers, and coaches, however, may not be so forgiving. This book was written not only to help the key people in your child's life understand the true nature of his social and emotional struggles but also to give your child a real chance for social success.

Our program is clinically proven and based on the latest evidence-based research. Our aim, through this tested method, is to help your child overcome shyness, manage social anxiety or withdrawal, and improve the quality of his or her family and peer relationships. Along the way, we'll help you enhance your child's assertiveness, confidence, enthusiasm, and empathy, as well as teach him or her to become increasingly flexible, tolerant, responsible, and respectful toward others.

How to Use This Book

You may recognize your child's characteristics in one of our real-life stories. More typically, however, your child will share features with many of the children described in our real-life stories. For this reason, read chapters 1 through 3 first to get a deeper understanding of your child's social struggles. Using our checklists at the end of each of these chapters, you can then identify the specific features of your child's social anxiety, withdrawal, or vulnerability most in need of change. In chapter 4, we'll help you understand the difference between teasing and bullying, the different types and dynamics of bullying, and some of the signs that may indicate your child is being bullied. Later in the book, you'll be able to determine if your child is most at risk for being neglected, rejected, or both by his or her peers.

In chapters 5 through 8, we provide step-by-step guidance regarding how to help your child overcome shyness, manage social anxiety or withdrawal, and improve the quality of his or her peer relationships. You will then be able to select relevant treatment goals, and design and implement an individualized program of coping strategies and social skills for your child. Finally, chapter 9 will help you make sense of your child's progress and determine whether professional help (and possibly medication) may be warranted. You can also take advantage of our recommended resources at the end of each chapter.

Please note that for ease of reading we have alternated our use of masculine and feminine pronouns from one chapter to another. So, in chapter 1, we use masculine pronouns when referring to the child; in chapter 2 we use feminine pronouns; and so on.

How This Book Can Help You

Helping Your Socially Vulnerable Child is intended to be used in several ways. It may be utilized as a step-by-step guide for parents who have not yet sought professional help; as an educational resource about the nature, development, and treatment of social and emotional struggles in children and adolescents; or as a source of support when you are deciding whether or not professional help is warranted. For best results, we encourage you to utilize the book in addition to working with a qualified therapist.

Helping Your Socially Vulnerable Child can also serve as a valuable resource for other family members and relatives, mental health professionals, teachers, school psychologists and administrators, learning specialists, speech and language pathologists, occupational therapists, and others who are interested in better understanding and helping children overcome their social challenges.

Are you ready? Let's get started. First, we'll figure out the specific nature and extent of your child's shyness and/or social anxiety.

1

When Your Child Is Shy
or Socially Anxious

I can't go to the tennis match. What if I throw up?

—Beth

What if I make a mistake? No one will like me.

—Stephen

Chapter Objectives

In this chapter you will learn to:

- Recognize the key types of shyness or social anxiety in children

- Understand some of the reasons why your child may be shy or socially anxious

Living in an Intimidating World

Think about it. We live in a world that can be very intimidating. It's quite natural to feel shy or self-conscious in some situations. Confrontations with family, friends, or coworkers can potentially occur every single day of our lives. Do you ever dread any of these encounters? Do you at times become overcome with worry or feel sick just thinking about getting together with a difficult relative? Fortunately, for most of us these feared social situations are few and far between. For the socially anxious child, however, even ordinary interactions can be intimidating. Routine encounters that we often take for granted, like starting a conversation, joining a group, or asking someone for help, can be major challenges.

Shyness and social anxiety often begin in childhood but can go unaddressed until early adolescence. How can you tell if your child's social anxiety is not just a passing phase? If his anxiety has lasted for six months or more, is disrupting school, peer, or family well-being, or is now leading to other problems like depression or social withdrawal, it may be a longer-term issue that requires assistance or treatment.

Research shows that untreated social anxiety in adolescence is often associated with school dropout, depression, alcohol abuse, and lower satisfaction with occupational and social relationships (Albano and Detweiler 2001). For these reasons, the time to intervene is now. The first step is to recognize the key features of your child or adolescent's social anxiety.

What Does Shyness or Social Anxiety Look Like?

All children experience social anxiety in their own unique way. Most socially anxious children and adolescents, however, share some key features, including shyness, self-consciousness, performance anxiety, and a fear of negative evaluation. We will discuss the characteristics of each type of social anxiety and then illustrate them with a real-life story.

Reluctance to Participate in Unfamiliar Situations

You may have noticed that your child needs considerable warm-up time before participating in new or unfamiliar social situations. The time frame can range from a few minutes before joining a birthday party to many months before participating in a karate class. For some children, simply thinking about a playdate with an unfamiliar child or attending a soccer match for the first time can be overwhelming.

You may have always thought of your child as shy and respected his need for warm-up time. In addition, you may have found it easy to appreciate your child's quiet nature, since shy children are more likely to be kind and respectful toward others and less likely to experience behavioral problems. You may have noticed, however, that because your child needs so much warm-up time he is not progressing in social and extracurricular activities at the same rate as his peers, even though he may be quite outgoing and confident at home with family and/or neighborhood friends. Remember, shyness is about getting acclimated to new or unfamiliar social situations. In our experience, a shy child may behave in the following ways in new encounters:

- Warms up slowly

- Remains alone

- Clings to caregivers

- Speaks softly

- Becomes easily overwhelmed (cries, freezes, or has tantrums)

- Resists trying new activities

- Needs to observe first before participating

- Hesitates to start or join a conversation

- Blushes easily, hides, looks down, or covers face with hands

- Falls apart when interacting with two or more children

We illustrate some of the characteristics of socially anxious children in our real-life story of Isabelle and her parents, Karen and Liam.

■ Isabelle's Story

Isabelle is a sweet, sensitive, and shy seven-year-old girl. She loves to play outside with her dad, Liam, and her best friend, Lilly, from her neighborhood. But when two or more children come over to play, Isabelle often becomes overwhelmed and confused. Isabelle is also reluctant to try any new activity. She initially gets very excited when Karen mentions an upcoming birthday party or playdate. As the event gets closer, however, Isabelle cries and shuts down. She usually does attend these events, but she generally clings to Karen and minimally participates only after considerable warm-up time and reassurance.

Isabelle loves soccer. However, despite having her father as a soccer coach, Isabelle stays on the sidelines, watching her teammates for most of the game. When she is finally ready to play, she is often upset to find out that the game is nearly over.

Isabelle is very bright and looks forward to going to school. Her teacher reports that she is quiet and obedient and usually plays with only one other child. When Isabelle is called on during class, she often covers her face with her hands, blushes, or looks down.

Concern About What Others Are Thinking

As children get older, they start to pay more attention to what others think of them. So, in addition to taking a cautious approach to new situations, some children may be self-conscious. You may have noticed this in your child—he may seem fearful of being the center of attention, perhaps worrying about making a mistake or looking stupid.

Your child may have trouble relaxing or tend to hold himself back in academic, social, or extracurricular situations. He may not only worry too much about what others think, but he may also be overly critical of his own behavior. This can be frustrating to both the child and the parents, especially if he actually does well in school, sports, or social situations. In addition, at home you may see a child who is funny, comfortable, and confident. You may wish that he wouldn't worry so much and could be a bit less intense about making mistakes. In our experience, self-conscious children may feel apprehensive in any of the following social situations:

- Participating in social or extracurricular activities

- Getting called on in class

- Writing on the blackboard

- Reading or speaking in front of people

- Eating in front of others

- Using public bathrooms

- Asking for help

- Getting dressed in front of others

You can see some of the characteristics of self-conscious and socially anxious children in our real-life story of Stephen and his parents, Walter and Lorraine.

■ *Stephen's Story*

Stephen is a bright, pleasant, and kind ten-year-old boy who does well in school, enjoys playing sports, and has many friends. But Walter and Lorraine remark that Stephen constantly worries about making mistakes and is extremely hard on himself. Stephen won't raise his hand in school even if he knows the answer. During baseball games and karate competitions, Stephen holds back and performs less well than he does during practices. If he makes one mistake on a spelling or math test he shuts down and cries.

Stephen is very sensitive and wants everyone to like him. His feelings get hurt easily, especially if he thinks others are mad at him. He is terrified of getting into trouble at school. Walter and Lorraine are becoming concerned. Outwardly, their son is an achievement-oriented success, but privately Stephen is weighed down with self-doubt and low self-esteem.

Fear of Failure

We all dread performance-based situations at one time or another, fearing that we will faint or embarrass ourselves in an important job interview, for example. Somehow, we manage to muddle through these situations and emerge relatively unscathed. Fortunately, we don't find ourselves facing these kinds of challenges too often. For some children and adolescents, however, the fear of failure is so strong that they completely avoid performance-based situations. Simply thinking about these situations may trigger panic in these children.

You may have noticed that your child or adolescent is giving you a hard time about participating in specific academic, social, or extra-curricular activities, such as the following:

- Taking tests

- Participating in musical or dramatic performances

- Participating in athletic events

- Giving oral presentations

- Attending gym

- Attending group meetings

This reluctance to participate may be hard for you to understand, especially if your child generally does well on tests or in sports. You probably encourage your child to simply try his best and avoid over-emphasizing his performance. Yet, despite your efforts to minimize his performance-related pressure, he may still feel physically sick before math tests, for example, and try to avoid them.

Some of the characteristics of children who experience strong social or performance anxiety can be seen in our real-life story of Beth and her parents, Alan and Amy.

■ Beth's Story

Beth is a quiet, pleasant, and responsible eleven-year-old girl. She does well in elementary school, is liked by her peers, and is a gifted athlete. Most academic and athletic activities come easy for Beth, with the exception of competitive tennis play.

Although she is still in elementary school, Beth was recently asked to join her local middle school tennis team. During practice, Beth plays with tremendous confidence and often beats much older players. In competitive play, however, Beth often feels physically sick, worries about vomiting, and fears losing. Alan and Amy are concerned because Beth is refusing to play in any more tournaments and she is thinking about quitting the team.

Fear of Humiliation

Social and performance anxiety can disrupt a child or adolescent's school performance, peer interactions, and/or family well-being. But it's important to keep in mind that most children like Beth are typically well adjusted, especially if the social and performance anxiety is limited to one or two situations. For some children and adolescents, however, the social and performance anxiety becomes so widespread that it affects virtually every area of their lives. Any kind of social situation that involves a potential confrontation is either endured with tremendous anxiety or is avoided altogether.

Perhaps you have noticed that your child or adolescent refuses to participate in social and/or extracurricular activities. In fact, even obligatory situations like school may be avoided when social and performance situations (like tests, oral presentations, or gym class) are scheduled. Your child or adolescent may also make every effort to avoid family outings, especially to public places like shopping malls or restaurants. And if you push too hard, he may freeze, panic, or have an explosive outburst.

You may have always hoped that your shy child would outgrow his social fears, and you may now be concerned that he is developing social phobia (which encompasses a wide range of social or performance situations and a general fear of being embarrassed or humiliated). In our experience, children and adolescents with social phobia may have any of the following fears or personality characteristics:

- Shyness

- Self-consciousness

- Social and performance anxiety

- Fear of negative evaluation

- Fear of being recognized or scrutinized

- Fear of being the center of attention

- Self-focused

- Fear of rejection

- Phobic avoidance

Notice that social phobia can include features of each type of social anxiety. As a result, social phobia typically affects more areas of social functioning and causes greater disruption to social, academic, and family well-being than other forms of social anxiety do. You'll see some of the characteristics of children and adolescents with social phobia in our real-life story of Paul and his parents, Stephanie and Arthur.

Paul is a soft-spoken, thoughtful, and sensitive thirteen-year-old boy. He is an excellent student and has a number of good friends. However, he is terrified of being the center of attention and becoming embarrassed or humiliated; he often thinks that everyone is scrutinizing him. Paul is very sensitive to the physical feelings in his body, reporting frequent headaches and needing to go to the bathroom all the time. Lately, Paul has been refusing to go to unfamiliar places (for instance, shopping malls, restaurants, movie theaters) with family or friends because of the possibility of having a panic attack or doing something embarrassing.

Some Reasons for Your Child's Social Anxiety

Thus far, we've discussed the different types of social anxiety. You may even recognize many of your child's behaviors in our real-life stories. What may be harder to understand, however, is why your child continues to be socially anxious when he has experienced few humiliating social experiences. You may have noticed from our real-life stories that social anxiety is often sustained by unpleasant physical feelings and/or worry about negative evaluations.

Uncomfortable Physical Feelings

Let's imagine for a moment that you have been asked to speak at your child's school. Which feelings would concern you the most? Would you worry about feeling tense and anxious, getting sick, or others noticing that you're tense and anxious? Of course, none of these outcomes is ideal. To some degree, however, you can expect to feel a bit uncomfortable before and during your talk. Almost all of us would feel this way; we just wouldn't want anyone to notice.

Children with social anxiety often experience these uncomfortable physical feelings before and during feared social situations, including the following:

- Headaches, muscle tension, or tightness in chest

- Stomachaches, nausea, or fear of vomiting

- Shaking, sweating, or blushing

- Shortness of breath, dizziness, or heart palpitations

Young children may not always understand why they feel uncomfortable, and they may become afraid to feel this way. Older children and adolescents are more likely to make the connection between feared social situations and their unpleasant physical feelings. As a result, the child begins associating the physical discomfort with potential dreaded outcomes such as vomiting or having a panic attack. Thus, the *fear* of getting sick helps sustain the child's social anxiety.

For this reason, your child may be acutely aware of his physical feelings and any indication that others may be noticing his anxiety. Observable physical symptoms such as blushing or shaking may cause your child the greatest distress. But, more often than not, these signs of anxiety, such as sweating, are subtle and hard to recognize. What's important here is your child's perception of these physical feelings, which brings us to our next topic.

Worry About Receiving a Negative Evaluation

Let's go back to your talk at your child's school. In addition to being apprehensive about others noticing that you're nervous, which of the following would you be thinking about—making a mistake, forgetting what to say, or failing altogether? Even the most confident and skilled speakers may worry about potential negative outcomes. Their collection of personal experiences, however, helps them discount the potential likelihood of such thoughts coming true.

Children and adolescents with social anxiety are especially sensitive to hints of negative evaluation such as being criticized, judged, or teased. Research has shown that socially anxious youth have a tendency to focus on the negative features of social situations; overestimate their chances for failure, embarrassment, and ridicule; and minimize their own abilities to cope (Kearney 2005).

The actual outcome is not so important here; it's how your child interprets the outcome that is meaningful. Your child's evaluation of feared social situations will depend on the following:

- The intensity of the physical feelings

- The extent to which these physical feelings can be recognized by others

- The strength of the child's beliefs in negative outcomes

- The child's perception of embarrassment

Like unpleasant physical feelings, negative evaluations can sustain a child's anxiety. But both may result in phobic avoidance of social situations. Up next, we help you understand how avoiding social or performance situations can interfere with your child's well-being.

Avoidance Due to Catastrophic Thinking

How would you feel if your proposed talk was rescheduled at the last minute because of inclement weather? Relieved? Grateful, since you know it would have been a disaster? Many people think this way. However, these social or performance situations are never an actual disaster. In fact, we often perform better than expected. Thinking about possibly being embarrassed or humiliated is the hardest part. But when your child or adolescent manages to avoid dreaded social situations, in his mind embarrassment, humiliation, or ridicule have been prevented. As a result, he will be even less likely to confront his social fears in the future.

Social anxiety is by nature irrational because there is little evidence to support one's fearful beliefs. Each of our real-life stories differs regarding the type of social anxiety and the degree of phobic avoidance experienced. What's similar, however, is that the children and adolescents never really experience negative social outcomes—they just fear such outcomes.

So, what can we do? Telling them not to worry is of little help. Having your child confront and feel the fear is the only way to help your child overcome his anxiety. Yes, he will become anxious. But his anxiety will lessen as soon as he realizes that nothing terrible happened. But why is your child so fearful of social situations in the first place? It's because he is afraid to get anxious.

Fear of Being Afraid

No one wants to feel uncomfortable. Even adults, who may recognize that the chances of being embarrassed in social or performance situations are low, still dread feeling embarrassed. Being afraid of these feelings is what causes your child's social anxiety to spiral out of control.

An important part of our program is to help your child accept his social anxiety as a part of who he is. This means becoming increasingly open to thinking about and experiencing his socially anxious feelings. Of course, this is no easy task. Your child may not only be afraid to feel this way but may also truly believe that embarrassment or ridicule is unavoidable. For this reason, if encouraged to confront feared social situations, he may experience strong avoidance reactions. Does your child engage in any of the following behaviors before or during social confrontations?

- Temper tantrums or explosive outbursts

- Crying, freezing, or panicking

- Pretending to be sick

- Hiding in bedroom or bathroom

- Refusing to speak at or go to specific activities or places

If so, these behaviors may seem manipulative to you. What's really going on, however, is that your child is showing you that he is overwhelmed and will do anything to avoid feeling this way. These acting-out behaviors are actually survival tactics rather than willful acts of disobedience. In chapters 5 through 8, we'll show you how to effectively respond to your child's avoidance reactions and promote his social confidence.

Origins of Your Child's Social Anxiety

Now that you have a better understanding of the workings of your child's social anxiety, we can discuss its origins: research suggests that social anxiety is the result of biological, psychological, family, and peer influences (Barlow 2002)—which are seen in the child's temperament and environment.

Your Child's Temperament

Your child may have always been shy or overly fearful. He may have started out as a fussy baby, become wary of strangers, and remained cautious in approaching new people or situations. These behaviors are related to your child's temperament or personality. Research suggests that children with such behaviorally inhibited temperaments are more likely to develop anxiety problems in general and social anxiety in particular (Kagan, Reznick, and Snidman 1986). It's as if your child's brain is wired to be overly alert to signs of danger, whether present or not.

At this point, you may have accepted that your child is prone to experiencing social anxiety, but you may still wonder where this tendency came from, especially if you're an outgoing and socially confident individual. On the other hand, you may have always been shy or socially anxious and worry that your child will struggle with this too. Either way, it's no one's fault. Chances are that you, your spouse, or a close relative experiences biological sensitivity of some sort, often expressed in the form of worry, panic, sadness, or some other form of social anxiety (for instance, shyness, self-consciousness, or social phobia).

Sometimes, we may feel like our children inherit our best and worst features. It's easy to dwell on the negative aspects of your child's social anxiety. But your child's emotional sensitivity also means that he is loving, warm, and affectionate. Be assured that there is no reason why he cannot develop into a socially confident young adult, particularly with your love and support and active efforts to help promote his socialization skills.

Through the Eyes of Your Child

Your child's temperament sets the stage for the development of social anxiety. This usually takes the form of unpleasant physical feelings, and difficulty adjusting to unfamiliar social situations. Research has also shown that children with social anxiety are susceptible to errors in thinking. These errors are referred to as cognitive distortions, which are based on faulty assumptions and may cause or, at the very least, sustain a child's social anxiety. Below, we illustrate some common cognitive distortions frequently referred to in the literature (Kearney 2005), using our real-life stories.

Personalization. The child sees negative outcomes as being his fault despite evidence that the opposite is true. For example, when her class loses recess privileges, Isabelle blames herself even though other children were misbehaving.

All-or-nothing thinking. The child views outcomes in extreme ways, such as good or bad, success or failure, or black and white with no gray areas.

Negative filter. The child emphasizes the negative aspects of the situation, so much so that he overlooks the "big picture." For example, Stephen, who does well in school and sports, thinks of himself as a failure when he makes a single mistake. Even when he does well, he still manages to find something negative to emphasize.

Catastrophic thinking.   The child assumes that the most negative and devastating outcomes will occur. For example, even though Beth plays with tremendous confidence during practice tennis sessions, at tournaments she fears the worst, such as vomiting or losing badly.

Fortune telling.   The child believes he can predict future (negative) outcomes. Paul, for example, avoids many social situations because he predicts that someone he knows will see him do something embarrassing and will tell his peers about it.

Mind reading.   The child believes that he knows what others are thinking, likely believing that they're saying negative things about him.

The socially anxious child's mind is like a wall of shame. Only the negative and embarrassing experiences, those in which he felt any social anxiety, are attended to and remembered. Even previous positive experiences may get discounted. This way of thinking makes your child or adolescent psychologically prone to experiencing further social anxiety. In chapters 5 through 8, we'll identify these errors in thinking so you can help your child learn to evaluate social situations in healthier and more realistic ways.

Your Family Environment

Your child's temperament and thinking patterns make him sensitive to the experience of social anxiety. Your family environment, however, may also play a role in sustaining his social anxiety. For example, Beth's mother, Amy, couldn't bear to see her daughter get so upset before and during each tennis match. As a result, she encouraged Beth to stay home in order to spare her from having a humiliating experience. And what loving parent wouldn't try to protect her child under these circumstances?

Paul's parents, Stephanie and Arthur, are soft-spoken, self-described "homebodies." Given that they both work full-time, Stephanie and Arthur rarely socialize, preferring a quiet family life. Thus, when

Paul started avoiding social activities, Stephanie and Arthur were not overly concerned.

What do these two different family environments have in common? Both families are unintentionally helping their children to avoid social confrontations. This can be problematic since the only way to overcome social anxiety is to confront and feel the fear.

We also have to watch what we say around our children. For example, when we emphasize the opinions of others or dwell on the negative, we can easily encourage, if not strengthen, our children's tendency toward negative evaluations. In chapter 5, we'll help you understand how parenting styles can contribute to your child's social anxiety, and we'll discuss effective parenting strategies that can minimize your child's phobic avoidance.

Please take a moment to complete the following checklist. Your answers will help you tailor our program to your child's specific needs in chapter 5.

Checklist: My Child's Social Anxiety

1. The key features of my child's social anxiety include:

    ☐ Shyness

    ☐ Self-consciousness

    ☐ Social or performance anxiety

    ☐ Easily embarrassed or humiliated

2. My child's social anxiety is currently sustained by:

    ☐ Fear of getting sick

    ☐ Negative evaluations

    ☐ Avoidance of social situations

    ☐ Fear of getting anxious

3. Some factors that generally contribute to my child's social anxiety include:

☐ Behaviorally inhibited temperament

☐ Errors in thinking

☐ Overprotective family environment

☐ Peer relationships

4. My child's social anxiety disrupts his:

☐ Academic functioning

☐ Social and extracurricular activities

☐ Family well-being

☐ Peer relationships

Summary

In this chapter we have helped you understand the key features and possible causes of your child's social anxiety. Although the children depicted differ in the form of anxiety and degree of phobic avoidance, their peer relationships are largely positive. These children *desire* to be with their peers. Their social anxiety is irrational but, if managed, will likely not lead to other problems. In chapter 2, we will introduce three more children and their parents in real-life stories that will be referred to throughout the book to illustrate how to help your child. These children experience social anxiety as well, but they also struggle with social withdrawal. In other words, they choose to isolate themselves from both familiar and unfamiliar peers. We'll also discuss the nature of social withdrawal and its relationship to social anxiety and depression.

Recommended Resources

Kearney, C. A. 2005. *Social Anxiety in Youth: Characteristics, Assessment, and Psychological Treatment.* New York: Springer.

Markway, B. G., and G. P. Markway. 2005. *Nurturing the Shy Child: Practical Help for Raising Socially Skilled Kids and Teens.* New York: St. Martin's Press.

Anxiety Disorders Association of America, www.adaa.org

The Child Anxiety Network, www.childanxiety.net

2

When Your Child Is Socially Withdrawn

No one likes me. I don't know why.

—Ralph

I wish my mom would just leave me alone. I have enough friends and interests.

—Jessica

Chapter Objectives

In this chapter you will learn to:

- Recognize the key forms of social withdrawal in children

- Understand the relationship among social anxiety, withdrawal, and depression

- Recognize the many faces of childhood depression

Choosing Solitude

With our many work and family responsibilities, we may sometimes long for a few moments of uninterrupted solitude. But we expect children and adolescents to want to be with others. Thus, it may be hard for you to understand why your child chooses to be alone. Of course, there is nothing wrong with wanting to spend some time alone. Solitude can be a time for reflecting, getting organized, or simply resting and relaxing. But there may be other reasons behind a child or adolescent's social withdrawal.

As we discussed in chapter 1, many children with social anxiety want to be with their peers, but, because of shyness, self-consciousness, performance anxiety, or fear of humiliation, they avoid unfamiliar social situations. These children will avoid social interactions because of a fear of the discomfort that comes with social anxiety, leading to a cycle of avoidance that reinforces the fear, even if the anxiety is entirely irrational. However, there are other children who isolate themselves, or withdraw, from *both* familiar and unfamiliar people and situations, possibly stemming from an actual history of unsuccessful social interactions. Also, some children may withdraw from social situations, not because of overwhelming, irrational anxiety or a history of unsatisfactory peer interactions but simply because of a preference for solitary activities.

Preferring to Be Alone

You may have noticed that your child or adolescent has always been very good at keeping herself occupied. She has always preferred solitary activities such as playing in her room, doing homework, reading, and listening to music over getting together with others. Up to now, you may not have been overly concerned since she's always done well in school and has been well liked by her peers. Now, however, she is getting older and you may be worried about her tendency toward solitude. She appears too content to stay at home at a time when her peers are becoming increasingly involved in social and extracurricular activities. It may seem unnatural that she has so little interest in being with others. Even more baffling is the fact that she often does well during obligatory peer and family situations and even appears to enjoy them. In our experience, such children may demonstrate any of the following characteristics:

- Slowness to warm up

- Soft-spoken and reserved demeanor

- Social anxiety (mild)

- Preference for quiet and solitary activities

- Adequate peer relations

■ Jessica's Story

Jessica is a sensitive, soft-spoken twelve-year-old girl. She does well in school, enjoys playing noncompetitive sports, and is well liked by her peers. Yet Jessica likes nothing better than to be at home with her family.

When Jessica was younger, she participated in extracurricular activities and attended summer day camp. Now, however, Jessica spends the bulk of her free time in her room. She loves to read, listen to music, or surf the Internet. Her teachers describe her as a model student and popular among her peers. Her phone rings often and she appears to enjoy talking to her friends. Yet Jessica rarely gets together with her friends. Her mom, Ann, is having difficulty understanding why Jessica is so withdrawn. She is concerned that Jessica is becoming increasingly isolated. Her dad, Ron, is shy and fully expects that Jessica will eventually come out of her shell.

It's Easier to Be Alone

Jessica interacts well with her peers, but she lacks the desire to be with them on any regular basis. She simply prefers solitary activities. Some children and adolescents who choose to be alone, however, actually wish to be with others. They may avoid social situations because of shyness, self-consciousness, or social anxiety. More important, however, they may have a history of less-than-adequate social interactions with their peers. As a result, even though they want to be with others, they may have learned that it's easier to be alone.

You may have noticed that your child or adolescent strongly resists participating in both familiar and unfamiliar situations involving her peers and even family gatherings. Any attempts to push her to participate may result in prolonged temper outbursts. And while she may appear to be content spending all her free time watching television or playing video games, you know that she is bored and lonely and wants to be with others. You may feel as if you have to walk on eggshells around her, since she is so sensitive and takes even casual remarks very personally. She may never have had an easy time expressing her feelings.

As much as you want to help her, you don't know what to do. It breaks your heart when you see her with her peers. She simply doesn't fit in and she doesn't know how. Such children may display any of the following characteristics:

- Shyness

- Self-consciousness

- Social anxiety (mild to moderate)

- Refusal to participate in unfamiliar situations

- Reluctance to participate in familiar situations

- Difficulty expressing emotions

- Low frustration tolerance, and proneness to temper outbursts

- Less-than-adequate peer relations

Ralph's story, told below, is an example of the experience of a child who struggles in the presence of others.

■ Ralph's Story

Ralph is an introverted and irritable eleven-year-old boy. He does well in school but cannot accept constructive feedback from his parents or teachers. Ralph is not athletic, and he has never been interested in playing sports. Living in a sports-oriented town has been a major social disadvantage for him. Ralph refuses to participate in any extracurricular activities. His mom, Elaine, is always trying to find activities that might pique his interests. Yet, no matter what she does, Ralph ignores her efforts, makes excuses for not participating, or has temper outbursts. Ralph's dad, Len, tries to encourage him to do father-son activities such as playing golf and going to the movies. Len even volunteered to be a scout leader to encourage Ralph's participation in the local Boy Scouts troop. Ralph did attend a few times, but he stayed by himself and then refused to go back.

Elaine and Len are concerned that Ralph has few friends. When he's not doing his schoolwork, he plays video games constantly. Occasionally, Ralph plays with his eight-year-old neighbor, but only if the neighbor comes over. And his best friend, Tommy, is rarely around because of his involvement in sports. In addition, Ralph has difficulty expressing his emotions with words, and, when he does say how he feels, he tells his parents that everyone seems to be against him.

Choosing to Be Alone Because of Depression

Unlike Jessica, Ralph would like to be with his peers but withdraws because of his history of unsuccessful social interactions. Paul (see chapter 1) also wants to be with others, but he avoids unfamiliar social events because he becomes overwhelmed with anxiety. There are other children and adolescents, however, who may choose solitude because they are completely overwhelmed with social anxiety and are also experiencing depression.

For such a child, over time, the social anxiety begins to take on a life of its own and then pervades every potential social confrontation. The child dreads feeling like the center of attention, and she cannot help but feel different since she believes that everyone is scrutinizing her. The reality, of course, is that few people, if any, are actually paying very much attention to her. Ultimately, it is her anxious reactions such as blushing, freezing, or panicking that draw others' attention to her, reinforcing her belief that all eyes are upon her. Her constant alertness to others' conversations, facial expressions, and gestures exhaust her and rob her of the emotional and physical strength she needs in order to participate with others. She may eventually withdraw from interacting with her peers on any regular basis.

In our experience, as a child or adolescent becomes increasingly debilitated as a result of her social anxiety, she will also experience depression. And, unfortunately, the feelings of sadness, helplessness, and low self-esteem that stem from the depression can cause others to avoid her. In the next section, we will define depression and its many faces, and then we will examine the relationship between social anxiety, social withdrawal, and depression.

What Is Depression?

We all feel sad at one time or another, perhaps in response to family, marital, or work-related stress. These feelings are normal and we typically bounce back into the swing of our daily activities. Children and adolescents also experience transient feelings of unhappiness in response to disappointments in their lives such as earning a poor grade on a test, losing an athletic event, or misplacing a favorite toy. However, can a child really be depressed? The answer is yes, but it depends on how we define depression. There are three ways in which children experience depression: with a single, temporary symptom, with a group of symptoms, and as a disorder.

Most children and adolescents experience a single symptom of depression at one time or another, usually feelings of sadness or unhappiness. This symptom is typically temporary and not considered part of a larger problem.

Depression can also occur as a group of symptoms, often referred to as a "syndrome." Children and adolescents may experience sadness, fatigue, loss of interest in activities, and eating or sleeping difficulties as part of a depressive syndrome. Depressive syndromes are much less common than temporary single depressive symptoms and are typically triggered by major stressful life events such as loss of a loved one, parents' divorce, or chronic peer rejection.

Finally, depression may also be viewed as a disorder. For this to occur, children and adolescents must experience at least five symptoms every single day for at least two weeks. Characteristic symptoms include sadness, loss of interest in nearly all activities, irritability, fatigue, sleep problems, disturbance in appetite, feelings of worthlessness, guilt, and thoughts of death or suicide (American Psychiatric Association 2000). Depressive disorders cause significant interference in social, home, and school-related functioning. Depressive disorders in preschool and school-age children are rare (occurring in less than 2 percent of the population of this age group). During adolescence, however, depressive disorders range from 2 percent to 8 percent. In children and adolescents with other problems such as social anxiety or learning disorders (Strauss and Last 1993), rates of depression are often higher.

Defining a person's depression as a symptom, syndrome, or disorder is a relatively simple task. Recognizing depression in a child, however, represents a much greater challenge, partly because of how we generally think about depression. For example, it's widely accepted that common features of depression include the following:

- Sad or unhappy feelings

- Tearfulness

- Lack of energy

- Sleep and/or appetite problems

- Somatic complaints

But depression in childhood has many faces, and its form often differs depending upon the child's age and developmental level.

The Many Faces of Depression

Depression in children is often expressed as irritability or moodiness. Irritability is one of the most common symptoms, occurring in about 80 percent of youth who experience a depressive disorder (Goodyer and Cooper 1993). Other common symptoms in children include the following, which we may dismiss as being related to laziness, lack of motivation, or just choosing to be difficult:

- Indifference to parental requests

- Argumentativeness

- Inflexibility

- Low tolerance of frustration

- Difficulty tolerating daily routines

- Difficulty negotiating home- or school-based transitions

In addition, depression is often expressed in the form of separation fears, social withdrawal, or refusal to attend school in pre-school children. Academic and peer difficulties become increasingly common in depressed school-age children. Helplessness ("I can't do anything right"), guilt ("It's all my fault"), and negative self-statements

("Everything I do stinks") also begin to emerge at this time. As these feelings continue to develop in adolescence, increased social isolation, low self-esteem, and thoughts of death may result. Given the many forms of depression, it's not surprising that we often overlook or misinterpret the signs in young people. For this reason, it's important to pay attention to any noticeable changes in your child's behavior.

Recognizing Changes in Your Child's Behavior

Recognizing observable changes in your child's behavior that suggest depression is not always an easy task. But if your child is suffering from depression, in your heart you know that something is not quite right. The behaviors that you observe are not characteristic of your child. Perhaps her usual pleasant mood is now sad, irritable, or tearful. She may have lost interest in extracurricular activities or spends an inordinate amount of time in her room. She may have trouble falling or staying asleep or be waking up very early in the morning.

The above examples are relatively clear signs of depressive symptoms. More typically, however, changes in your child's behavior are more subtle or gradual. For example, you may have assumed that your child or adolescent was doing well in school, but then you come to find out that she's missed homework assignments and is doing poorly. Maybe your child has always been shy or withdrawn and rarely called her friends. But now, her phone doesn't ring at all and you cannot remember the last time she socialized with her friends. Perhaps your child has always been a finicky eater, but now she barely picks at her food. Or your child may have never been a high-energy individual, but recently she has been complaining of fatigue and takes regular naps during the day.

When you're trying to determine whether to seek treatment, evaluating such subtle changes in behavior can be tricky, since any of these behaviors could be short lived, a response to specific stressful situations, or even the result of other issues such as anxiety, physical illness, or relationship problems. For this reason, it's important to also look at the intensity, duration, and pervasiveness of depressive symptoms. For example, maybe your child has always been moody, irritable, and argumentative. Thus, it's not surprising when she reacts this way to your demands. But lately, she's been refusing to participate in even her own desired activities. In addition, you notice for the first time that her negative attitude is affecting her friendships. Or, she may have always been sensitive to the physical feelings in her body, but recently she's been spending too much time in the nurse's office or has been refusing to attend school. These behaviors are a departure from your child's ordinary manner and are therefore a cause for concern.

Some Causes of Depression

A child's or adolescent's depressive symptoms can be due to a wide range of factors. Like anxiety, depression can run in families. While heredity may play a role, depression often results from a complex interaction of biological, neurochemical, psychological, and environmental factors. Research suggests that depressive symptoms often accompany other problems, such as the following (Barnard 2003):

- Family matters such as divorce, remarriage, or sibling problems

- Medical or psychological problems in family members

- Hospitalizations

- Loss, relocation, or school-related changes

- Peer neglect and/or rejection

- Chronic anxiety

In this book, we are looking at depressive symptoms as a consequence of social anxiety and/or social withdrawal. What matters most is not the exact cause(s) of depression, which is often unclear, but its accurate identification and treatment. In any case, if you suspect that your child is experiencing symptoms of depression that are interfering with her well-being, immediately contact your child's pediatrician, school counselor, or qualified mental health professional. In chapter 6 we'll discuss how to treat your child's depressive symptoms, and in chapter 9 we'll help you with the decision to seek professional help.

When Social Anxiety, Withdrawal, and Depression Come Together

Your child or adolescent may be withdrawn, making no effort to initiate any social contacts or join any extracurricular activities. Perhaps she spends large amounts of time in her room, complains of tiredness, fatigue, and headaches, and has difficulty concentrating. Everything seems too much for her, from getting up in the morning to completing her homework at night. When asked to complete a chore, she politely agrees but never follows through. She refuses to attend school when performance situations like taking tests or oral presentations are inevitable. If she cannot avoid these situations, she responds with panic, tears, or explosive outbursts. She looks sad and listless and is becoming increasingly withdrawn. And lately, her gloomy outlook is affecting the mood of the entire family. Such children and adolescents often struggle with many of the following features of social anxiety and avoidance, social withdrawal, and depression:

Social anxiety:

- Shy/soft-spoken

- Self-conscious

- Performance anxiety/panic

- Fear of negative evaluation

- Social avoidance of particular situations, such as school, public places or restrooms, cafeterias or restaurants, and confrontations with peers, family, or school personnel

Social withdrawal:

- Few or no friends

- Limited involvement in family activities

- Lack of involvement in social or extracurricular activities

- Social isolation

Depression:

- Sad, irritable, or depressed mood

- Gloomy outlook

- Fatigue

- Somatic complaints

- Concentration difficulties

- Sleep or appetite problems

- Low or negative self-esteem

George is one such adolescent who struggles with significant social anxiety, withdrawal, and depression.

■ George's Story

George is a soft-spoken, overweight, and sensitive fifteen-year-old boy. He wears baggy clothes to hide his overweight body and rarely talks to his peers or teachers at school. When confronted by others, he blushes easily, looks down, or covers his face with his hands. George often skips gym class and never uses the bathroom at school. He stays by himself and is often seen wandering the halls aimlessly. On days when he has to take a test or do a group presentation, George refuses to attend school.

His parents, Beverly and Herbert, acknowledge that George has always been shy and a bit of a loner. But they're concerned that George is now taking long naps as soon as he comes home from school and is often still asleep when they get home from work around dinnertime. Although George has friends, he does not seem interested in pursuing any social contacts. And lately, George has been refusing to participate in family activities as well. He complains of headaches, nausea, and fatigue, looks sad and listless, and spends all his free time in his room.

The Costs of Social Withdrawal

Peer relationships are an important part of social and emotional development. Children learn unique skills from interacting with their peers. Sporadic avoidance of peer-related situations may limit opportunities for the development of social skills. Children may then have difficulty fitting in and then be more prone to being embarrassed. Persistent and widespread social avoidance can hamper the development of friendships and foster loneliness and low self-esteem. This is why it's so important to break the cycle of social avoidance before it leads to social withdrawal, depression, or isolation. Now, take a moment to complete our end-of-chapter checklist. Your answers will help you tailor our program (see chapters 5 and 6) to meet your child's specific needs.

Checklist: My Child's Social Withdrawal

1. The key features of my child's social withdrawal include the following:

    ☐ Preference to be alone

    ☐ Reluctance to be with others

☐ Refusal to be with others

2. My child's social withdrawal is currently sustained by:

☐ Social anxiety

☐ Social avoidance

☐ Depressive symptoms

3. My child's social withdrawal disrupts her:

☐ Academic functioning

☐ Social and extracurricular activities

☐ Family well-being

☐ Peer relationships

Summary

In this chapter, we have discussed the key forms of social withdrawal and its relationship to social anxiety and depression. Each of the children in our real-life stories chose to withdraw from their peers and/or family because (1) they preferred to be alone, (2) it was easier than interacting with others, or (3) being with others was simply too hard because of overwhelming anxiety and depression. In chapter 3, we'll introduce three more real-life stories that we will refer to throughout the book to illustrate how to help your child. These children also experience different degrees of social anxiety, withdrawal, and/or depressive symptoms. More important, however, these children, because of additional problems, have become *socially vulnerable*, which means that they are at risk for being neglected or rejected by their peers. We'll help you to understand the reasons behind your child or adolescent's social vulnerability.

Recommended Resources

Naparstek, N., and M. Wallace. 2006. *Is Your Child Depressed? Answers to Your Toughest Questions*. New York: McGraw-Hill.

American Academy of Child and Adolescent Psychiatry, www .aacap.org

American Psychiatric Association, www.psych.org

American Psychological Association, www.apa.org

3

When Your Child Is Socially Vulnerable

Why does Ira keep lying and making up stories? He knows the other kids won't tolerate it.

—Horace

Tracey can watch TV for hours but takes breaks every five minutes when doing her homework. She can be so manipulative.

—Florence

Chapter Objectives

In this chapter you will learn to:

- Identify the key types of social vulnerability in children

- Understand some of the reasons why children become socially vulnerable

- Recognize the specific features of your child's social vulnerability

The Importance of Friendship

Friendships, especially those early relationships formed in elementary school, have an impact that lasts well into our adult lives. It's not surprising that many of us still maintain close ties with our childhood friends. A peer group provides children with companionship, emotional and physical support, social comparison, and, most important, self-esteem. The need to feel valued, accepted, and part of a larger group is universal and begins early in life (Hartup 1992). Perhaps for this reason, the quality of childhood peer relationships is one of the best predictors of later success (or problems) in life (Asher and Parker 1989).

Think about how you feel at the end of a day when the stressors of life simply refuse to take a rest. How do you gather the strength to face the challenges that lie ahead, for example, when your family is not so understanding or available? You turn to your friends. Now imagine how life would be if you felt all alone, you didn't belong anywhere, and no one wanted you. Welcome to the world of the socially vulnerable child.

Becoming Socially Vulnerable

Children may withdraw from social activities and relationships for many reasons, including anxiety, fear of being embarrassed, or a history of negative interactions. Whatever the reason, when social anxiety or withdrawal leads to poor peer relationships there are usually additional problems involved. For instance, some children may be overly aggressive, impulsive, or hyperactive. Other children may not be socially savvy, may lack social skills, or may cry too easily. Ultimately, these children become socially vulnerable, which means they may be ignored, excluded, or, even worse, actively rejected by their peers. And it's not their fault. Why would a child intentionally alienate others or do things to compromise his ability to fit in? Most of these children not only are unaware of how their behavior alienates their peers but also have great difficulty understanding why they are not accepted.

Our purpose here is to help you understand the reasons why your child may have become socially vulnerable. In chapters 7 and 8, we'll show you some effective strategies to facilitate your child's social competence and confidence. Let's now look at the different types of social vulnerability.

Socializing Without Road Signs

As you may recall, most of the children in our real-life stories who experience mild to moderate social anxiety have friends and are well liked. Ralph's story is an exception. He is certainly not debilitated with social anxiety, so it seems that he should be doing better socially. Is he just taking the easy way out by withdrawing from peer interactions and family obligations? Let's revisit Ralph and his parents, Elaine and Len, to try to understand his behavior.

According to Elaine, Ralph is too serious and "takes everything personally." He doesn't seem to understand the difference between playful ribbing and meanness. In addition, asking him to do anything, such as homework or brushing his teeth, invariably results in a power struggle. If Elaine or Len gets mad at Ralph, he says, "You hate me." Len says that Ralph has very little tolerance for others' idiosyncrasies and always looks annoyed.

Ralph's teachers report that he tends to stay by himself and rarely initiates social interactions with his peers. They express concern about his know-it-all attitude and his difficulty admitting mistakes, receiving feedback, and accepting responsibility. For instance, if another child verbally teases him and Ralph retaliates with anger, he often says, "I didn't do anything wrong," and seems unable to understand his part in the altercation.

Elaine remarks that Ralph is very self-absorbed. If she's talking on the phone and cooking dinner at the same time, for example, Ralph becomes huffy if she doesn't drop everything and immediately help him with his homework. And when she tries to explain why he has to wait, he says she's "mean." Elaine keeps pushing Ralph to get involved in activities, but the harder she tries, the more withdrawn he becomes. Lately, Ralph has complained of aches and pains and feeling tired all the time. Elaine and Len are exhausted from these constant conflicts and they don't know how to help their son.

Why Is This Happening?

Imagine driving across the country and finding yourself in a place without any road signs. Let's also assume that no maps are available and, of course, that your car doesn't have a built-in navigation system. What do you do? You keep driving. You desperately search for any clue or landmark that might give you some sense of direction. Eventually, if you're like most of us, you'll give up, pull off to the side of the road, and call for help—but not before becoming overwhelmed with frustration, panic, or sheer exhaustion.

If your child is like Ralph, he may be socializing without any road signs—the subtle social cues that help us gauge the success of our interactions with others. Reading these cues allows us to understand and interpret other people's body language. Being able to read body language is extremely important, since 60 percent of communication is nonverbal (Nowicki and Duke 1992).

Facial expressions, eye contact, and the tone of one's voice are examples of social cues that help guide our interactions. Imagine talking to an old friend or colleague whose monotone voice and muted facial expression never changed in response to your laughter, sarcasm, or seriousness. You'd have a very difficult time trying to figure out what kind of impression you were making. In fact, you might even go overboard in your expressions and vocal tone in an effort to generate some kind of response. In the end, however, your well-intended efforts would likely make things worse and leave your friend annoyed.

Some children, because of their limited ability to pick up nonverbal cues, may misinterpret social situations, leading to negative reactions from their peers. Ralph, who has great difficulty understanding sarcasm, came home one day after school feeling very excited. He told Elaine that he had been picked last to play dodgeball, but that the last player, according to his peers, was the "best" player. He had missed the smirks on his teammates' faces as well as the rolling of their eyes. Understanding sarcasm requires an ability to read another's body language, but also the ability to interpret the meaning of words spoken in a specific context.

Some children, like Ralph, interpret language quite literally. For instance, when Ralph was being especially demanding one day, Elaine said, "Please stop. You're driving me crazy." Ralph became frantic, repeatedly yelling, "She called me crazy! Mom thinks I'm crazy." In another example, Len reported having the following exchange with Ralph:

Len: Ralph, when we get to the video store, you can pick out one DVD.

[*Ralph nods in response. At the video store counter, Ralph puts down one DVD, two video games, and a large chocolate bar.*]

Len: I said you could choose one *DVD* ...

Ralph: I did.

Len: You're not getting any video games or candy.

Ralph: You're mean. You hate me!

Len: That's it. We're going home!

It's easy to understand why Len would get upset in this situation. He views Ralph as spoiled, manipulative, and unappreciative. What's going on, however, is that Ralph actually feels gypped. His difficulty understanding the meaning of language precludes him from seeing his father's perspective, and it also prevents him from realizing that he needed to verbally express his desire for the candy bar and video games. Because of this difficulty with taking others' viewpoints, children like Ralph often accuse others of being liars.

One Sunday afternoon, Len asked Ralph if he wanted to accompany him to the library. As they got ready to leave, Ralph's younger next-door neighbor came over to play. Three hours later, it was time for dinner, but Ralph was insisting that Len take him to the library. Len tried to explain that the library was now closed and that Ralph had chosen to play with his neighbor instead. Ralph, however, called his dad a liar, insisting that Len had promised to take him, and then proceeded to have a meltdown.

So what's going on here? If your child is like Ralph, he may be struggling with some pragmatic learning issues (Lavoie 2005). *Pragmatics* is a term that refers to our ability to understand and use language and deals with both verbal and nonverbal communication. Children with pragmatic learning issues often have difficulty understanding and interpreting any of the following in other people:

- Humor

- Sarcasm

- Body language

- Facial expressions

- Moods

- Gestures

- Intent

Children with pragmatic learning issues may appear to be self-absorbed; for instance, they may be unable to see another's perspective. In addition, children like Ralph are frequently overly sensitive to criticism, tend to have a negative attitude, and have difficulty accepting responsibility for their actions and behaviors.

Sometimes parents and teachers find it difficult to believe that a child has learning issues when he is obviously intelligent and doing well in school. But learning challenges don't always emerge as academic problems, especially with intelligent children. Until the third or fourth grade, most bright children typically compensate for their difficulties in the academic arena, although subtle signs may suggest that they are struggling. For example, your child may receive fairly good grades but still have difficulty with one or more of the following:

- Handwriting and/or printing

- Reading comprehension (characters, plots, or settings)

- Abstract assignments (math, science, or writing)

- Information retention (complex information or basic facts)

- Visual-spatial tasks (tying shoes, copying from the blackboard, or walking in line without bumping into others)

As the academic material becomes more complex and abstract, often around fifth or sixth grade, your child may suddenly start to struggle in areas that were previously easy for him, such as math, science, and English. As a result, he may for the first time receive a poor grade. You may assume that such a grade resulted from a lack of effort. However, it's more likely due to your child's increasing struggles with pragmatic learning issues. For Ralph, academic issues were not yet evident. However, he continued to have difficulty writing script, tying his shoes, and remembering basic facts like the months of the year. These signs suggest that he may have yet-unidentified learning issues.

A child with pragmatic learning issues may also have difficulty taking information learned in one context and applying it in another. For instance, he may learn one concept in math class but be unable to apply a similar concept in science class. Similarly, a child may complete one math problem with ease, but when faced with another may struggle, refuse to try, or have an outburst. Such behavior is often viewed as willful or lazy. However, the child may simply be utterly exhausted from the continuous strain of dealing with his learning challenges.

However, our focus here is not about specific learning deficits in math, spelling, or reading. Rather, it's about how being "wired" differently can affect a child's ability to perceive, process, and interpret social situations.

If your child is like Ralph, you may have noticed that he does best interacting with one child at a time, preferably a low-key child who allows him to be in charge. When two or more children are involved, he may quickly become confused, feel overwhelmed with frustration, and ultimately withdraw from the interaction. This is because it's extremely difficult for him to follow and understand multiple social cues and conversations simultaneously. For this reason, your child is most at risk in unstructured and ambiguous social situations such as recess, gym, and lunch, and when he is entering and leaving the school grounds.

If your child or adolescent struggles with pragmatic learning issues, he may become socially vulnerable because of any of the following behaviors:

- Becomes easily frustrated

- Insists on doing things his way

- Accuses others of lying

- Is possessive regarding personal items

- Acts withdrawn, moody, or irritable

- Is overly anxious or controlling

- Has difficulty communicating wants and needs

- Has difficulty understanding rules in unstructured situations

- Fears getting into trouble

- Refuses to play sports or other group recreational activities

Pragmatic learning issues may be diagnosed by psychologists, speech-language pathologists, and/or neurologists. Data is typically collected from multiple sources, including child, parent, and teacher reports, as well as specialized tests. If you think that your child may be experiencing pragmatic learning difficulties, please consult a psychologist, speech-language pathologist, neurologist, or other health care professional.

Ralph knows that he doesn't fit in, but he doesn't understand why, so he simply withdraws from his peers. Some children, however, believe that they do fit in and should even be popular with their peers. Despite this, they keep doing things to alienate their peers, such as being too loud, impulsive, or silly. Unlike Ralph, who withdraws to protect himself, these children continue to put themselves "out there" and get actively rejected.

Violating the Rules of the Road

On the road, if we drive too fast or neglect to pause long enough at a stop sign, we may be cited for a moving violation. In social situations, children who are "always on the go," cannot stop fidgeting, or have trouble restraining their actions may receive social citations from their peers for being overly annoying, demanding, or inappropriate. Such a child may quickly acquire a negative reputation, setting the stage for his being isolated, ostracized, or victimized. Family members as well may have difficulty tolerating the constant barrage of challenging behaviors. Let's meet Ira, one such child, and his parents, Horace and Rena.

■ *Ira's Story*

Ira is a friendly, affectionate, and outgoing ten-year-old boy. He loves to play sports and run around outside. His mom, Rena, remarks that Ira is very intense and loud.

Ira also gets frustrated easily and has frequent explosive meltdowns, often saying things like "I hate you," especially when his parents set limits for him. Fifteen minutes later, however, he is all smiles again, as if nothing ever happened. Even so, Rena and Horace often resent his inappropriate behaviors.

Horace is also concerned about Ira's constant fidgeting, tapping, and spinning. He wonders why Ira dances, skips, and slams his feet rather than just walking in the house or going upstairs like everyone else. Further, Ira often reads upside down and moves his feet under the table during meals. As if that's not enough, Ira is also an incredibly finicky eater, "freaks out" when he hears loud noises, and cannot stand to be in places with very bright lights.

Ira is very rough with his affections. For instance, if Horace is reading the newspaper on the couch, without warning Ira will fling his body onto Horace. Ira is also too rough with his four-year-old brother, David, and cannot keep his hands off him. For this reason, both Rena and Horace are afraid to leave Ira alone in a room with his younger brother.

At school, Ira's teacher is concerned that he constantly "calls attention to himself." During lessons, Ira frequently blurts out the answers, interrupts, hides under his desk, refuses to try, and shuts down when he makes a mistake. He'll often have a meltdown and call himself an idiot or say that he hates himself. Despite being very bright, he often rushes through his assignments and makes careless mistakes. During group assignments, Ira is often left without a partner. When the teacher assigns another student to work with him, that person often complains.

Ira reports being bullied frequently, saying that the other kids are always trying to get him into trouble, such as putting their belongings under his chair and then accusing him of stealing them. If Ira tells the teacher, the other kids brand him a "tattletale" or band together to say he's lying. During lunch he's forced to sit alone and other children dump their garbage on his tray; at recess his peers refuse to let him play. On the bus, the other kids push him, call him names like "stupid" and "retarded," and shoot rubber bands at him. Ira also says that the kids from his block are afraid to be seen with him; they'll play with him around the neighborhood but not at school.

Rena and Horace don't know what to do. They feel terribly sad because Ira is having such a hard time. But they're not sure what to believe, because, they say, Ira constantly "lies, makes things up, or repeatedly changes his side of the story." It doesn't help that Ira's teacher says he's just immature and needs to learn some self-control, and that the guidance counselor says, "Boys will be boys."

Why Is This Happening?

If your child is like Ira, he may struggle with some hyperactive and impulsive behaviors. Hyperactive behaviors include incessant talking; frequent fidgeting, tapping, spinning, or swirling; and difficulty playing quietly. Impulsive behaviors include interrupting or blurting out thoughts, having difficulty waiting, rushing through schoolwork, and having trouble keeping his hands to himself.

A child with Ira's behavioral profile may get diagnosed with attention-deficit/hyperactivity disorder (ADHD). A child with ADHD may struggle primarily with inattentiveness, primarily hyperactive and impulsive behaviors, or both. In Ira's case, hyperactive and impulsive behaviors were disrupting his class and alienating him from his peers. However, the fact that your child is experiencing some symptoms of hyperactivity and impulsivity doesn't mean that he has ADHD. Many other problems or conditions may mimic ADHD. For example, did you know that children with sensory integration issues often look hyperactive and/or impulsive?

Children with sensory integration issues have a hard time taking in and processing sensory information. For this reason, they may be over- or undersensitive to the range of sensory stimuli (Biel and Peske

2005). Let's take a closer look at Ira's behaviors to see which ones may be better explained by sensory processing issues. For instance, what's the story with Ira's constant tapping and fidgeting movements?

Ira's constant movements may be due to his body's inefficient processing of sensory information. As a result, he craves constant stimulation, which is likely satisfied through his bodily movements as well as his "annoying" behaviors (for instance, making noises, acting silly, and touching others). Other behaviors that suggest sensory processing issues include Ira's finicky eating habits (taste), strong affection needs (touch), and oversensitivity to bright lights and noise (sight and hearing). If your child has sensory processing difficulties, he may have other sensory issues, such as sensitivity to clothing tags and seams.

A child with sensory processing issues is not just being "difficult." Rather, he is doing his best to make sense of the myriad confusing sensory experiences in his world. Because of the way his central nervous system is wired, he may not know how to respond to specific sensory stimuli. For example, Ira keeps forgetting to use an "inside voice." Why does he keep forgetting? Is he being manipulative? What's likely happening is that because of inefficient sensory processing Ira can neither gauge nor regulate the loudness of his voice. To him, his voice sounds fine. He cannot understand why his mother keeps bothering him about it. In another example of Ira's difficulty with particular stimuli, he cannot tell the difference between an accidental bump and an intentional offense. According to witnesses at school and home, the collisions are typically accidental. Yet Ira believes they are always intentional, responds as if he is badly hurt, and often retaliates with anger. This is because he feels the sensation of touch much stronger than the average child does. Understanding and responding to sensory stimuli are simply more difficult for Ira. If you believe that your child is experiencing significant sensory integration issues, consider consulting a respected occupational therapist in your area.

Ira is also experiencing some impulsive behaviors that could partly be explained by sensory processing issues, anxiety, or temperamental intensity but are more characteristically associated with ADHD-like symptoms. These include his tendency to interrupt, blurt out his thoughts, and rush through his schoolwork. If Ira's impulsive symptoms are due to ADHD, it probably means that the portions of his brain responsible for inhibition and self-control are underactivated (Barkley 2005). This means that he has a limited ability to stop himself from engaging in inappropriate behaviors. (ADHD may be diagnosed by psychologists, psychiatrists, and/or neurologists following comprehensive evaluations that include data from child, parent, and teacher reports as well as formal testing.) Whatever the cause, children experiencing sensory integration issues, or hyperactive and/or impulsive behaviors, may appear to be immature (emotionally and socially), demanding (needs a lot of attention or supervision), difficult (must do things their way), lazy or unmotivated (rushes through schoolwork), manipulative (lies, keeps doing forbidden things), or hypochondriacal (cries easily, frequently claims being hurt).

Lying and making up stories is another of Ira's behaviors that alienates other kids and confuses the adults in his life. He desperately wants to fit in, so why does he continue to say things that aren't true? Ira's storytelling is the product of his impulsivity; any thought or idea that pops into his head gets expressed. Most of us come up with occasional far-fetched thoughts and ideas, but we also have the ability to think them through and use our judgment when deciding to alter the facts, especially when we want to avoid hurting another person's feelings. Ira does not have such an ability.

Ira also desperately wishes things were a certain way, and because he has trouble waiting or can't make these things happen he may quickly start to believe his wishes are true. For example, recently some of the other kids at school were talking about how "cool" guns were. Ira interjected that his dad made guns for a living. Of course, this is the farthest thing from the truth—Horace is an accountant. But Ira kept talking about his dad's gun-making business. He so desperately wanted to be accepted that at that moment he really believed this to be true. Questioned by an adult a few minutes later, Ira remembered saying that his father makes guns, but he did not know why he said such a thing. In other, similar situations, he might not even remember saying it at all (and would therefore seem to be lying again).

As you can see, it can be difficult for parents and even the child to distinguish between manipulative, intentional lying and the type of impulsive storytelling that we see with Ira. How can you tell the difference? If your child is like Ira, he feels very guilty and remorseful afterward. It's not something he likes or wants to do; he just does it.

For now, however, you can help your child by first identifying the behaviors that are making him socially vulnerable. Children who struggle with sensory integration issues and/or hyperactive or impulsive behaviors may become socially vulnerable by doing any of the following:

- Violating others' personal space (cannot keep hands to themselves)

- Interrupting or blurting out (cannot wait)

- Acting silly

- Exhibiting "weird" behaviors (making noises, belching, picking nose)

- Lying or making up stories

- Crying or becoming easily frustrated

- Needing to be the "center of attention"

- Acting in an overly annoying and loud manner

- Being very particular about things like food and clothes

- Fearing loud or bright stimuli such as fire drills and bright lights

- Frequently falling or bumping into things

Now, we'll discuss a third type of social vulnerability. This time, it's not about missing social cues or being hyperactive and impulsive. Rather, it's about a seeming inability to focus, pay attention, and be organized.

Socializing While Distracted

Imagine spending several hours getting your family ready for a weekend excursion. You've made your lists, packed carefully, and even double-checked that everything was in order. Amazingly, you're ahead of schedule and all set to go. Now, where are your keys? We all know how frustrating this situation can be, especially when so much thought and planning were involved. But what if you didn't have a list, you became distracted when a friend called, and you even forgot that you were leaving for vacation today? What would your spouse or partner say?

The above scenario illustrates the daily lives of children with attention issues. These children are easily distracted, forgetful, and always losing things, rarely paying attention to relevant details. As a result, their interactions with family, peers, and school personnel can become quite strained. Let's meet Tracey and her parents, Florence and Scott.

■ Tracey's Story

Tracey is a quiet, intense, and agile nine-year-old girl. A gifted athlete, she is on the softball, basketball, and gymnastics teams. She thinks about nothing else. Her mom, Florence, wishes that Tracey would put even half this effort into her schoolwork. She has a great deal of trouble focusing on schoolwork and is very disorganized. Tracey often forgets to bring her books home from school, misplaces her assignments, and doesn't remember when she has tests coming up. Getting her to do anything independently, such as homework or chores, is one big struggle.

When Tracey finally sits down to do her work, she takes breaks every few minutes, yet she can watch television or play video games for hours without stopping. Tracey can be so focused during the activities that she likes that she often fails to respond when her name is called. Florence sometimes wonders if Tracey has difficulty hearing, but then

Tracey hears just fine other times, such as when her parents are in another room discussing private matters that are of no concern to her. Florence cannot help but feel that her daughter's behavior is manipulative.

Tracey's third-grade teacher describes her as very bright and capable, but she is concerned that Tracey doesn't take pride in her work. For example, Tracey makes careless mistakes, looks for shortcuts, and often leaves her work incomplete. In addition, Tracey has trouble finding the needed materials for each subject, partly because her desk is a complete mess.

During lessons, Tracey gets distracted easily, particularly when the other kids are making noises or fooling around. She often looks annoyed and responds with an angry grimace. Her teacher says that Tracey needs to "listen better" when directions are given in class, and sometimes she has to hear the directions three or four times before she understands assignments. She also forgets to write down her assignments in her notebook, which is filled with creative doodles. Tracey often looks confused, becomes frustrated, and puts her head down, but she still refuses to ask for help.

Tracey's dad and softball coach, Scott, is concerned that his daughter is starting to lose interest in playing sports and is withdrawing from her friends. He says he cannot help but notice that Tracey is no longer playing "with all her heart." She used to keep careful track of her teammates' progress, but now she often appears uninterested in following the game. She never knows the score and always looks surprised when it's her turn to bat. Recently, Tracey's teammates became very upset with her when an easy grounder got past her in the outfield. By the time she realized where the ball was, the other team had scored and won the game.

Tracey seems to be having trouble fitting in with her peers. She either follows the other girls around or quickly withdraws from the interactions. When her parents ask

her about her difficulty with social interactions, Tracey
says that she doesn't know what to say to other kids. Scott
is concerned that his daughter is becoming increasingly
withdrawn and looks fatigued all the time. He worries that
there's more to Tracey's social withdrawal than her shy and
quiet personality.

Why Is This Happening?

If your child is like Tracey, you may notice that attention problems are a main area of concern. Examples of Tracey's inattentive behaviors include the following:

- Forgetfulness

- Losing things

- Taking frequent study breaks

- Making careless mistakes

- Lack of attention to detail

- Incomplete assignments

- Taking shortcuts

- Disorganization (desk, backpack, bedroom)

- Distractedness

- Trouble following directions

- Difficulty listening

A child with frequent symptoms of inattention that interfere with his home, school, or social functioning may receive a diagnosis of attention-deficit/hyperactivity disorder, inattentive subtype (ADD) by a psychologist, psychiatrist, and/or neurologist, after comprehensive evaluations that include child, parent, and teacher reports. However, parents often have difficulty accepting that their child really has

ADD. After all, how is it possible for Tracey to be so focused when playing video games but unable to concentrate for more than five or ten minutes at a time when studying? Children with ADD can pay attention, especially if the task at hand is stimulating. In fact, research shows that children with ADD are no more distracted than children without ADD during activities like watching television or playing video games (Barkley 2005). The inattentiveness becomes apparent, however, during boring or tedious tasks like schoolwork. Thus, children with ADD have trouble *sustaining* their attention during tasks that are less stimulating to them.

So it's not that Tracey is manipulative, lazy, unmotivated, or irresponsible. Rather, she struggles with a pattern of inattentiveness that affects many areas of her life, including her sense of time. Children with ADD live in the here and now. For Tracey, five minutes is as difficult to envision as five hours. As a result, when Florence tells Tracey that dinner will be ready in five minutes, Tracey is not likely to immediately wrap up the activity she's involved in and come down to the dining room. Instead, she'll likely hear the direction but not really take it in or respond to it.

Because of Tracey's poor sense of time, she also has great difficulty accepting no as a response to her requests. Many times when a parent says no they simply mean not now, maybe tomorrow. But kids like Tracey live entirely in the moment, and so they cannot envision anything about tomorrow. To them, "no" means "never." Understandably, Tracey often has meltdowns when she is told she can't have what she wants. And doing so in public does not endear her to peers, teachers, or coaches.

Some children with attention issues may also struggle socially because of their tendency to interrupt others' conversations. Here, it's not so much about being impulsive. Rather, these children interrupt due to a fear of forgetting what they wanted to say. Because they live completely in the present, they know that when the moment is over their thought may cease to exist. This is especially likely to happen if they weren't paying attention to the people and things around them in the first place. This is why many children lose things and forget about assignments and tests.

Children with ADD are believed to have trouble with their brains' executive functioning skills. These skills include planning, time management, working memory, organization, and problem solving (Dawson and Guare 2004). Working memory is the length of time we can hold information in our minds while simultaneously performing different tasks, and it also relates to the ability to connect past and current experiences. A child like Tracey is likely to quickly forget past unpleasant social experiences and thus not understand why her peers may not be so friendly anymore. Finally, Tracey's difficulty keeping her bedroom, school desk, and backpack in any kind of coherent order is likely due to her poor organizational skills.

Of course, every child who experiences inattentive behaviors does not have ADD. ADD is often misdiagnosed since other problems such as anxiety, learning challenges, medical problems, sleep difficulties, or depression also commonly result in inattentive behaviors. Sometimes, what looks like ADD is the result of central auditory processing (CAP) difficulties.

Children with CAP difficulty have trouble processing and understanding sounds. This is not an actual hearing difficulty. Rather, it's an inability to differentiate similar sounds, words, voices, or the location of sounds (Hamaguchi 2001). For children with CAP difficulties, listening is like trying to decipher an important answering machine message left by a caller with a thick accent, with a lot of static and noise in the background. Children with CAP have trouble making out words, following directions, or understanding conversations. This is especially true in noisy settings such as school or sports activities. CAP is more about having difficulty processing sounds than it is about having trouble paying attention. (CAP is typically diagnosed by audiologists and/or speech-language pathologists following a comprehensive evaluation.)

Let's take a closer look at Tracey's behaviors to see which ones may be better explained by CAP. Examples include:

- She appears to have a "hearing problem."

- She is easily distracted by noises.

- She acts annoyed when her peers are fooling around.

- Others feel that she needs to "listen better."

- She has difficulty following and understanding directions.

- She looks confused (doesn't "get it").

- She quickly withdraws from conversations.

Children for whom CAP difficulty is the primary issue can sustain their attention, especially if the task at hand does not require active listening and the setting is quiet. Children with CAP may also have difficulties with spelling, speech, and/or reading comprehension.

To complicate matters, however, many children, like Tracey, have behaviors consistent with both ADD and CAP. Thus, making sense of their struggles is no easy task. Children with attention and/or processing issues may appear to relevant adults as lazy, unmotivated, irresponsible, disorganized, disrespectful, scattered, forgetful, overly withdrawn, or anxious.

Children who struggle with inattentive behaviors and/or auditory processing issues may become socially vulnerable by doing any of the following:

- Making careless mistakes (schoolwork, sports, projects)

- Looking confused

- Not understanding directions or rules

- Acting angry, annoyed, or overly critical

- Seeming unfriendly

- Becoming frustrated easily

- Acting impatient

- Appearing sloppy

- Interrupting

- Behaving in a controlling manner

The fourth type of social vulnerability we'll discuss comes from social awkwardness and chronic inflexibility with others.

Socializing Without Flexibility

Imagine driving in the right lane and coming up to a red light. You recall a "no turn on red" sign being posted at this intersection in the past, but it seems to have been taken down. The car in front of you turns right at the light, but, still believing that you're not allowed to make a right turn on red at this intersection, you wait for the light to turn green. The drivers of the cars behind you are honking furiously, but you remain stopped at the light. Cars are now starting to go around you on the left in order to turn right in front of you, but you don't move forward until the light turns green. You later learn that your town's traffic engineers decided to remove the "no turn on red" sign at this intersection, having determined that it was no longer necessary. Still, you plan to refrain from making a right turn on red each time you approach this light in the future.

The above situation represents the kind of scenario experienced by some children who may have a wonderful memory for facts but, because of their rigidity, have difficulty conforming to social norms. We introduce you to Jeremy and his parents, Russell and Gail.

■ *Jeremy's Story*

Jeremy is a reserved, aloof, and ambitious twelve-year-old boy. He is a dedicated student and aspires to be a world-renowned scientist. His mom, Gail, expresses concern that Jeremy spends an unusual amount of time alone studying in his room, developing Web sites on his computer, or building

Star Trek *spaceship models in the basement. Jeremy seems
to know "everything" about* Star Trek, *and somehow he
manages to make every conversation, writing assignment,
and school project connected to this show in some way. His
memorabilia collection is so extensive that there is no longer
any room to walk around in the basement.*

*Russell says that Jeremy is the worst backseat driver
imaginable. Jeremy has memorized many of the maps,
locations, and landmarks of the United States, and his sense
of direction is uncanny. Yet Jeremy refuses to let his dad find
his own way. If Russell doesn't give in and go the way Jeremy
wants him to go, he often explodes, kicking the driver's seat,
screaming obscenities, or throwing his sneakers.*

*Jeremy's rigidity is not limited to traffic directions.
When Jeremy gets frustrated with his schoolwork, especially
abstract writing assignments, he refuses offers of help from his
mother by growling at her. At school, Jeremy rarely makes
mistakes. However, on the few occasions when he needs to
be given feedback, he nods politely and then refuses to make
corrections. He insists that he is right.*

*nJeremy has minimal interest in his peers. His teachers
remark that Jeremy tends to stay by himself, rarely looks at
others when talking to them, and often sighs or rolls his eyes
when observing or interacting with others. Jeremy is often
teased and called names such as "Trekkie," "geek," or "freak."*

*Gail is concerned that Jeremy's sloppy appearance isn't
helping him socially. His hair is often uncombed, his clothes
seem unkempt, and he often wears the same pants several
times per week. And he often forgets to brush his teeth or
take a shower. Gail wants to take him shopping to buy
some more-fashionable clothes in an effort to help him fit in
better, but Jeremy doesn't care. He seems oblivious to how
others see him.*

*Gail has noticed that Jeremy avoids talking on the
phone. In fact, if he must answer the phone, he seems
panicky and his hands flutter before he picks it up. If a*

classmate calls about a homework assignment, Jeremy passes on the information in an unemotional way and then hangs up quickly.

Gail says that Jeremy lacks the "empathy gene." He very rarely smiles or expresses any emotion, except when he is experiencing an outburst. In fact, overwhelmingly positive or equally distressing news typically result in the same muted expression. Both Gail and Russell express concern that Jeremy doesn't know how to relate to people. When Jeremy does interact, he talks at people rather than with them. He doesn't seem to understand why others are not as interested in Star Trek *and geography as he is, nor does he get why they continue to be rude to him.*

Gail and Russell are concerned about Jeremy's lack of desire to be with his peers (and his family). They feel that he should be with others. He has a dry sense of humor and at times appears to enjoy being with his peers. Classmates do occasionally call him, but despite Gail's encouragement Jeremy rarely calls back or follows through with social activities. Gail and Russell just want to help their son get connected in the real world and develop some lasting friendships.

Why Is This Happening?

If your child or adolescent is like Jeremy, he may struggle with some social relatedness problems, which are typically associated with disorders along the autism spectrum. For example, your child may appear to be self-absorbed, rigid, immature, temperamental, and socially awkward or withdrawn. Jeremy's behavioral profile is most consistent with one of these autism spectrum disorders, known as Asperger's disorder. Asperger's is a neurobehavioral disorder in which a child's intellectual and cognitive functions remain intact, but his social interaction abilities are significantly impaired (Lockshin, Gillis, and Romanczyk 2005). Asperger's may be diagnosed by psychologists, psychiatrists, and/or neurologists following comprehensive evaluations.

Jeremy exhibits many of the key characteristics of Asperger's, including limited social and emotional reciprocity, extreme rigidity, special interests (such as *Star Trek* and transportation routes), poor hygiene, and repetitive motor movements (hand fluttering). Jeremy also has difficulty understanding social cues and the unspoken rules of social interactions, both of which are also characteristics of Asperger's. As you may recall, Ralph has similar difficulties, which are the result of pragmatic learning challenges. Given the frequent overlap of these two neurobehavioral problems, and the fact that Asperger's is more widely studied, children are often misdiagnosed with one or the other (Stewart 2002). And, complicating matters further, a third condition known as nonverbal learning disorder (NLD) has been identified. Children with NLD also demonstrate social deficits and anxiety, along with fine- and gross-motor concerns and math difficulties. These children have intact language skills and their difficulties stem more from visual-motor and perceptual skill deficits (Tanguay 2001; Stewart 2002).

Of course, not every child with social-relatedness difficulties is struggling with Asperger's, NLD, or pragmatic learning challenges. The child's temperament, anxiety, and social needs can easily contribute to social problems. For example, children with strong-willed, "difficult" temperaments are often viewed by others as stubborn and inflexible. We regularly hear parents, teachers, school personnel, and coaches say, "He is just being oppositional." And, while this may be true, it may be more than a matter of temperament—it could be the result of the interactions between social anxiety, temperament, and additional complicating factors such as Asperger's, NLD, or pragmatic learning difficulties.

Social anxiety is evident to some degree in all of our real-life stories. You'll recall that Jeremy becomes anxious and panicky when talking on the phone. But if he is not interested in what others think about him, then why would he be anxious during these interactions? Perhaps his indifferent attitude toward others is his way of avoiding uncomfortable social situations. In this way, social anxiety plays its part in his social vulnerability.

Finally, in determining the reasons behind a child's social difficulties, we need to view their challenges in relation to their social needs. For example, neither Jeremy nor Jessica (see chapter 2) has strong social needs. Yet Jessica is popular and well adjusted, despite her desire to spend time by herself. Thus, Jeremy's social difficulties cannot be fully explained by his preference to be alone.

Because of these factors, the child may become socially vulnerable by doing any of the following:

- Making poor eye contact

- Acting withdrawn, moody, or irritable

- Looking angry, annoyed, or unfriendly

- Having a condescending attitude toward others

- Being rigid and inflexible

- Becoming frustrated easily

- Seeming naïve

- Appearing disheveled

- Performing odd behaviors or motor movements

- Focusing on unusual interests

- Acting annoying and rude

- Lacking friends

The Triple Threat

As you can see, there are many layers that contribute to a child's social vulnerability. It can start with your child's temperament, whether he is strong willed and "difficult" or slow to warm up and "passive." The second layer is your child's sensitivity to anxiety. As a child's social anxiety heightens, he will feel more out of control. The third layer is the child's neurological wiring, which can cause his internal world to become increasingly confusing, chaotic, and overwhelming. As a result, his social anxiety, social withdrawal, and natural temperamental disposition will become more pronounced (for instance, he may become increasingly oppositional or withdrawn). Regardless of their social vulnerability type, because of these three layers, the children described in this book all struggle with anxiety, withdrawal, anger, or fatigue.

Our focus here is not on diagnosing disorders, which can be very complex (and require comprehensive evaluations) because many disorders share common behaviors but have completely different origins. Rather, our focus is to help you identify the key behaviors that may cause your child to become socially vulnerable. Please take a few minutes to complete our social vulnerability checklist. Use the checklist to identify and monitor your child's problematic behaviors. In chapters 7 and 8, you'll also use this checklist to help you choose specific treatment strategies to facilitate your child's social success.

Checklist: Social Vulnerability

Please check any of the items below that are characteristic of your child or adolescent.

1. Personality

    ☐ Serious

    ☐ Self-absorbed

    ☐ Strong willed

    ☐ Passive

    ☐ Overly demanding

    ☐ Aloof

    ☐ Very particular regarding food, clothing, and so on

- ☐ Rigid or inflexible
- ☐ Bossy or controlling
- ☐ Lacking in empathy
- ☐ Overly sensitive

2. Attitude

- ☐ Conceited regarding his knowledge
- ☐ Disrespectful
- ☐ Condescending
- ☐ Angry or hostile
- ☐ Irresponsible
- ☐ Negative
- ☐ Spoiled or unappreciative

3. Social Awareness

- ☐ Misses social cues
- ☐ Has difficulty understanding consequences of actions
- ☐ Has difficulty understanding humor or sarcasm
- ☐ Acts naïve
- ☐ Has difficulty with perspective taking
- ☐ Is unconcerned about appearance

4. Activity Level

- ☐ Always on the go
- ☐ Fidgets
- ☐ Performs spasmodic movements
- ☐ Is easily fatigued

☐ Talks incessantly

☐ Has difficulty playing quietly

5. Impulsive Behaviors

☐ Cannot keep hands to self

☐ Has difficulty waiting

☐ Interrupts

☐ Blurts out

☐ Invades others' personal space

6. Attention Span

☐ Is easily distracted

☐ Has difficulty sustaining attention

☐ Is hyperfocused during preferred activities

☐ Has difficulty listening

☐ Has trouble following directions

☐ Forgets

7. Work Habits

☐ Seems lazy or unmotivated

☐ Rarely takes initiative

☐ Is disorganized

☐ Rushes through assignments

☐ Frequently fails to finish

☐ Does not pay attention to detail

☐ Is uncooperative

8. Self-Control

    ☐ Is easily frustrated

    ☐ Has explosive outbursts

    ☐ Is aggressive toward others

    ☐ Frequently cries

    ☐ Is unresponsive

    ☐ Is unpredictable

9. Socially Undesirable Behaviors

    ☐ Lies

    ☐ Accuses others of lying

    ☐ Has difficulty sharing

    ☐ Acts silly

    ☐ Is rude

    ☐ Is manipulative

    ☐ Calls others names

    ☐ Calls attention to self

    ☐ Has bad habits (picks nose, sucks thumb)

    ☐ Makes poor eye contact

    ☐ Perseverates

    ☐ Performs odd behaviors or movements

    ☐ Is clumsy

Summary

In this chapter, you have learned how to identify and understand the key types of social vulnerability. In addition to experiencing social anxiety and/or withdrawal, each of the children from our real-life stories also struggles with some underlying neurological issues that lead them to miss (or misinterpret) social cues, exhibit hyperactive or impulsive behaviors, be easily distracted, or become chronically inflexible. In chapter 4, we discuss the relationship between the types of social vulnerability and specific bullying behaviors. We will help you understand the difference between teasing and bullying, the dynamics of bullying, and your child's risk for being neglected and/or rejected.

Recommended Resources

Barkley, R. 2000. *Taking Charge of ADHD.* New York: Guilford Press.

Biel, L., and N. Peske. 2005. *Raising a Sensory Smart Child: The Definitive Handbook for Helping Your Child with Sensory Integration Issues.* New York: Penguin Books.

Hamaguchi, P. A. 2001. *Childhood Speech, Language, and Listening Problems: What Every Parent Should Know.* New York: John Wiley & Sons.

Kranowitz, C. S. 2005. *The Out-of-Sync Child: Recognizing and Coping with Sensory Processing Disorder.* New York: Skylight Press.

Lavoie, R. 2005. *It's So Much Work to Be Your Friend: Helping the Child with Learning Disabilities Find Social Success.* New York: Simon and Schuster.

Ozonoff, S., G. Dawson, and J. McPartland. 2002. *A Parent's Guide to Asperger's Syndrome and High-Functioning Autism.* New York: Guilford Press.

Stewart, K. 2002. *Helping a Child with Nonverbal Learning Disorder or Asperger's Syndrome.* Oakland, CA: New Harbinger Publications.

4

Understanding Bullying Behavior

If I could wish for anything
A better golfer I would be
I'd play tennis better than Pete Sampras
I'd do my homework without being asked
I'd be smarter than Albert Einstein
But, the thing I'd wish the most for would be
For kids to stop bullying me.

—Ira

Chapter Objectives

In this chapter you will learn to:

- Identify the key types of bullying behaviors

- Understand why socially vulnerable children are often blamed for being bullied

- Recognize when your child is being bullied

It's a Bad, Bad, Bad World

Bullying is often viewed as a normal part of growing up; this is the origin of the saying "Boys will be boys." Bullying in the school-age years is even deemed by some to be a necessary "rite of passage" into young adulthood. However, there is nothing normal or necessary about bullying. Instead, it is destructive to everyone involved.

Large-scale surveys suggest that nearly 6 million American school-age children are involved in regular acts of bullying in some form (Nansel et al. 2001). Equally disheartening is the news that 160,000 students miss school each day due to bullying, 25 percent of school-age children are bullied daily, 10 percent of school-age children are bullied weekly, 77 percent of youth have been bullied at some point during primary or secondary school, and 93 percent of school-age children have witnessed an act of bullying (Smith and Sprague 2003; Walker, Ramsey, and Gresham 2004).

These statistics are indeed alarming considering that bullying behaviors have both short- and long-term consequences for all involved parties. For example, victims of persistent bullying are more likely to experience a wide range of social, emotional, and academic difficulties, including the following:

- Anxiety, worry, and somatic complaints

- Sadness, social withdrawal, depression, suicidal thoughts or attempts

- Concentration difficulties, academic failure, or school refusal

- Anger, resentment, or explosive outbursts

- Physical injuries

- Confusion, insecurity, and low self-esteem

Long-term studies suggest that many of these problems persist into young adulthood, especially anxiety, depression, and low self-esteem (Olweus 1993).

Bullies have been found to have their share of later problems as well. For example, when bullies are allowed to engage in aggressive behaviors without interventions from adults, vandalism, shoplifting, truancy, and substance abuse become all the more likely when they are older. In fact, one long-term study showed that 40 percent of school-age bullies were convicted of three or more criminal offenses by age twenty-four (Olweus 1995).

Bullying is not something that should be taken lightly. It can start early and, if allowed to continue, can have devastating effects on young people. Many of us have been bullied at one time or another. And of course, bullying is not limited to the school grounds, nor does it necessarily cease with adulthood. Bullying occurs in work and family settings as well, and it can take the form of subtle negative comments or actions. Bullying behaviors diminish our self-worth, and they can create discomfort or dread whenever we think about or interact with the bullying individual. The problem, however, is that most people have their own (often inaccurate) idea of what constitutes bullying behavior. Below we'll examine the many forms of bullying, but first let's look at one behavior that is sometimes equated with bullying but is often distinct from it: teasing.

Teasing

It's important for both parents and children to be able to distinguish teasing from bullying. And there are several features that differentiate the two. Teasing typically involves two people of equivalent power. This means that both parties are similar to each other in their physical size, strength, and peer popularity. In addition, teasing usually occurs sporadically, with no intent to harm, and within the context of friendship. If a child says "I was only teasing" or "It was just an accident" but that child cannot be considered a friend of the person being teased, her intent is too often malicious and her actions may be identified as bullying.

The line between teasing and bullying can easily become blurred with a socially vulnerable child. The child's perception of the situation plays an important role here. For example, a child who cannot tell the difference between playful teasing and bullying may interpret (or misinterpret) any casual remark as having hostile intent. If she becomes upset by the interaction for any reason and other children continue to "tease" her, their intent can no longer be viewed as innocent.

Bullying

Bullying can be easily distinguished from teasing for many reasons, including how often it occurs. In most cases, bullying occurs frequently, sometimes relentlessly, with every intention of hurting the victim in some way. Teasing may happen only occasionally, and in a positive context or environment.

Further, unlike teasing, bullying involves a clear imbalance of power between the involved parties. Bullying can occur with just two children (bully and victim), but it is more likely to involve several children acting against one. Most children can handle altercations with a sibling or one other peer. However, no child can be expected to handle situations where a group of several children (or, in some cases, an entire class of students) "gangs up" on one child. Dan Olweus and his colleagues describe how the "bullying circle" permits, sustains, and reinforces bullying behaviors as a group phenomenon (Olweus 1993; Olweus, Limber, and Mihalic 2000).

Typically, one or two children (bullies) identify, target, and bully a weaker, less popular victim. Contrary to what you might expect, bullies are usually not unpopular and may have two or three friends who help fuel the bullying in both active ways (followers) and passive ways (supporters). The followers, referred to as "henchmen," who carry out the bully's malicious intentions, do not start the bullying on their own. Thus, both the bully and follower have limited power in isolation, and need each other to sustain the strength of the bullying circle. Weakening their connection is an important part in alleviating peer problems. The supporters, often a larger group of children, may encourage the bullying behaviors in a less obvious way. These children, often not so popular themselves, may smirk, giggle, and secretly enjoy seeing another peer being tormented. Collectively, this group contributes to the victim's perception that large numbers of children are actively harassing her.

Outside the bullying circle are the bystanders and the defenders of the victim. A bystander may dislike the bullying but choose not to get involved because she fears being ostracized or making things worse, or simply because she doesn't know what to do. Ira's friend Joe, who was aware of Ira's experiences with being bullied and feared becoming a victim himself, actually said, "I can't talk with you at school or sit next to you on the bus." Yet Joe is perfectly willing to come over after school for a playdate.

Both active and passive roles in the bullying process encourage and strengthen bullying behaviors. Doing nothing creates a social climate in which bullying is seen as acceptable. The defenders, though often small in number or nonexistent, can play a powerful role in weakening the bullying circle. Bullies often prey on socially vulnerable, "friendless" children who cannot retaliate. Having a best friend, especially one who will stick up for her, not only reduces the child's likelihood of being bullied but also minimizes the behaviors' negative impact. For this reason, if your child is vulnerable to being bullied, helping her develop the skills necessary to forge reciprocal friendships is vital.

Peer friendships are also important buffers against bullying because these behaviors often take place below the radar of adults, who may believe that bullying only involves physical acts like hitting or kicking. Bullies typically use verbal threats of physical force to intimidate their victims into feeling helpless and powerless. Psychological tactics such as ignoring or excluding the victim from peer group activities, spreading harmful rumors, or hurtful name calling in many ways are not only more emotionally damaging but also harder for teachers and school personnel to detect. Below, we describe the messages that bullying behaviors can communicate and the different kinds of these behaviors.

"You're Weak"

"I'm stronger than you" and "I can or will hurt you" are some messages that the physical bully conveys to her victims. Physical bullying typically occurs in the form of direct physical contact, for instance, hitting, spitting, shooting rubber bands, or destroying personal belongings such as school materials, clothing, or lunch items. Physical bullying, which is more characteristic with boys than with girls, can easily trigger fear, anxiety, and feelings of dread in the victims. Most bullies who resort to these tactics do so to threaten or intimidate, without intent to cause actual physical harm. The threat of physical aggression (saying "I'm going to throw you against the locker," along with a mild push or shove) is more than enough to cause victims to view school and other settings as unsafe and unpredictable. More rarely, however, a child or adolescent may intend to cause actual physical injury. Naturally, these situations are far more serious for both the bully and the victim, since bullies who use physical aggression at an early age are more likely to exhibit antisocial behaviors across the life span.

Physical Bullying

Ira is clearly a victim of physical bullying. His peers engage in the following behaviors toward him:

- Dumping garbage on his tray at lunch

- Destroying his clothes by placing ketchup on his seat

- Ripping his homework assignments

- Stealing his school materials

- Hiding his school books

- Trying to hurt him during gym

- Shooting rubber bands at him on the bus

- Extorting his lunch money

■ Pushing him in the school hallway and kicking him under the desk

"You're Worthless"

"You're stupid, ugly, and a loser" is the basic message that a verbal bully conveys to her victims. In some ways, verbal bullying can be worse than physical bullying, since verbal bullying attacks the child's personal qualities. Sure, sticks and stones may break our bones, but name calling is anything but harmless, especially to an overly sensitive or socially vulnerable child.

Verbal bullying can be extremely emotionally damaging. If it occurs too frequently, children are in danger of believing these hurtful messages. Verbal bullying is associated with anxiety, depression, loneliness, low self-esteem, and school refusal behaviors, and it is the most common form of bullying. This is not surprising since it's so hard for adults to detect: it's the bully's word against that of the less-popular victim. Who is the adult going to believe? Typically, neither the victim nor the bystander will report bullying behaviors. The victim may fear being branded a tattletale or worry that adult involvement will make things worse, and bystanders may fear the consequences of their reporting the bullying, namely that they will become victims themselves. Hence, verbal bullying persists, gradually eroding the self-worth of the victim through either direct or indirect behaviors.

Direct verbal bullying (actual interactions) can occur in person, on the phone, or even on the Internet. Sometimes the harassment is limited to one specific attribute, such as the child's intelligence ("stupid"), athletic ability ("klutz"), or appearance ("ugly"). While these insults are indeed emotionally damaging, there is hope that a child's overall self-worth may be preserved if she feels successful in other areas. Other times the harassment centers on the child's entire character or personality, with global insults such as "loser." These are harder for a child to handle since they attack the child as a person.

Indirect verbal bullying occurs in the form of malicious rumors spread about the victim. As we all know, rumors need not be true in order to catch on, and once they begin to spread, like a disease, the damage is done. Negative reputations soon follow.

Indirect verbal bullying is often how bullying becomes a group process. The bully counts on not only the support of her followers but, more important, the inability of the victim to defend herself. Given that verbal bullying is the most common kind of bullying behavior, it's not surprising that each of the socially vulnerable children described in this book experiences it to some degree.

Verbal Bullying

Both Ira and Jeremy are victims of direct verbal bullying, largely because they stand out. Ira's hyperactive and impulsive behaviors call attention to him, and Jeremy's unusual interests, behaviors, and unkempt appearance make it hard for others not to notice him. Ira finds himself being called "stupid," "retarded," "a loser," "gay," and "a klutz," and Jeremy gets labeled "a Trekkie," "a geek," and "a freak."

All of the socially vulnerable children in our real-life stories also experience indirect forms of verbal bullying. Ira is told he "has cooties," is "a tattletale," is "a liar," "steals," is "a crybaby," and "has no friends." Bullies say that Ralph is a "know-it-all," "never says sorry," is "a downer," acts "too serious," and is "angry all the time." Tracey is called "forgetful," "spacey," and "in her own world." Jeremy is labeled "weird," "smelly," and "a psycho."

"No One Likes You"

"You have no friends" and "Stay away from us" are some messages that the relational bully conveys to her victims. These messages are the most hurtful of all and can devastate the self-worth of any child. Of course, no one can get along with everyone, and this is perfectly fine. But to feel like no one wants us and that we don't belong anywhere is overwhelming. The goal of relational bullying is to reject, exclude, and ultimately isolate the victim so that she feels helpless and vulnerable. Relational bullying can easily destroy the victim's friendships. This may happen when a bully sours another child's reputation ("Don't play with her—she's weird"), steals friends, discourages neutral bystanders from getting involved, makes it difficult for possible defenders to come to the victim's rescue, and conspires with others to get the victim into trouble. Relational bullying is more characteristic in girls than boys.

The socially vulnerable child is especially susceptible to relational bullying. Because she so desperately wants to belong and cannot always tell who her friends are, she may misconstrue any neutral or fickle peer's actions as indicating friendship. As a result, she may repeatedly become a victim of manipulation ("I won't be your friend unless ...") and not understand why. Socially savvy bullies may also pretend to be her friend simply in order to bait her. Relational bullying is often subtle and very difficult to detect, and it is associated with peer rejection, anxiety, depression, loneliness, and acting-out behaviors. Like verbal bullying, relational victimization is evident in each of our real-life stories.

Relational Bullying

In addition to experiencing both physical and verbal bullying, Ira is also the victim of relational bullying. Ira's peers engage in the following behaviors:

- Picking him last during gym activities

- Refusing to let him sit at the "cool" table during lunch (forcing him to sit alone)

- Refusing to let him join games at recess

- Accusing him of stealing, cheating, and swearing in an effort to get him into trouble

- Spreading malicious rumors that he is gay, is retarded, and picks his nose

- Complaining loudly in class when forced to be his partner during activities

- Using hostile gestures (drawing a finger across the throat to mean "You're dead," or making a thumbs-down sign) to keep other kids from talking to him

- Excluding him from birthday parties and social events (so that often he is the only child in the class not invited)

Tracey's relational victimization is more subtle; her peers are not actively rejecting her. Rather, they have stopped going out of their way to invite her to playdates, parties, and sleepovers. Since Tracey is quiet and rarely takes initiative, she is beginning to feel left out. Tracey's peers feel uncomfortable about her commitment to sports, lack of social sophistication, and forgetfulness. Because of their discomfort, they refer to her as "Spacey Tracey" behind her back.

Ralph's experience is a bit different: he feels as if he is being rejected by his peers, but what he doesn't understand is that his peers' initial withdrawal is in response to his overly critical nature. Thus, he has learned to play it safe by withdrawing first.

Jeremy is being victimized in person and behind his back. But Jeremy's indifference to his peers helps to protect him since he doesn't care what they say or think. If your child is overly sensitive, like Ira, Tracey, or Ralph, see chapters 7 and 8 for advice on how to help her accept and manage her sensitivity to minimize the effectiveness of peer victimization.

The Role of the Victim

Educators and school personnel often label socially vulnerable children as "immature" or "social misfits." You may have been told that if your child were just to "stop calling attention to herself," "take responsibility for her actions," or "learn some self-control," the bullying would end. So where do these attitudes come from?

Some socially vulnerable children exhibit a wide range of behaviors that irritate others, such as being overly annoying, disruptive, or inappropriate; emotional, anxious, or aggressive; or active, impulsive, or restless. These children may be identified as *provocative* victims, and they are usually actively disliked. Because of their behaviors, it's almost unspoken that bullying these children is acceptable, or even deserved. This is one reason why few educators, school personnel, and peers will come to such a child's defense.

Ira is considered a provocative victim. Because of his hyperactive and impulsive behaviors, even his parents found him overly demanding and frequently lost their patience with him. And, while it may be true that provocative victims can contribute to their own bullying problems, this in no way legitimizes the harsh treatment they receive. It's not the child's fault. If she could exercise better self-control, she would. No child intentionally aims to alienate her peers. Remember, bullying is about an uneven distribution of power. Bullies have allies; the socially vulnerable provocative victim usually does not. Because of this, the child needs more support, not less.

The *passive* victim, on the other hand, does little to provoke being bullied. Her tendency to be anxious, insecure, unassertive, socially withdrawn, depressed, submissive, or afraid to get into trouble is what makes her an easy target. Moreover, because of these tendencies, educators and school personnel are often unaware of bullying toward passive victims.

The passive victim is most likely to be the recipient of verbal and/or relational bullying. Both of these forms of bullying are extremely difficult to detect, especially if executed by socially savvy bullies. Because the bully is rarely held accountable, the passive victim is indirectly blamed for being bullied. If she tells, no one believes her. If she overreacts, she gets into trouble. Thus, she learns to give in to the bully's demands, which not only sustains the bullying but also causes her to resent school personnel and no longer trust them as a source of support. Even when bullying behaviors are identified, the socially vulnerable child is less likely to receive help because of the complex and confusing nature of her difficulties.

For instance, although Ira is a provocative victim, his impulsive fabrications and constantly changing versions of bullying incidents lead teachers and school personnel to disbelieve him and dismiss his complaints. They view his lying as a bad character trait rather than a product of his neurological profile.

Socially savvy bullies also take advantage of Ira's oversensitivity to touch and claim that intentional physical altercations were just an accident. It doesn't help that his teachers rarely witness the bullies' provocations but never miss his "overreactions" to both accidental (for example, another child bumping into him in the hallway) and intentional physical acts. In their view, each situation is simply another example of Ira's tendency to call attention to himself and does not require intervention.

Ralph has difficulty getting help because of his misinterpretations of peer situations. His concrete and literal way of thinking make it difficult for him to see other children's points of view. It doesn't help that he takes everything personally, is easily annoyed, and refuses to accept responsibility for his behaviors. It's understandable that his teachers readily favor the reports of his more popular, socially savvy peers.

Jeremy, on the other hand, is also a victim of verbal and relational bullying. However, Jeremy is not interested in what others think. As a result, Jeremy may not be as socially vulnerable as Ira or Ralph, but his future is at risk if his social-relatedness skills do not improve. Tracey is also at risk for experiencing anxiety, loneliness, social withdrawal, and depression. However, unlike Ira and Ralph, who make some noise in order to be "heard," Tracey's quiet and withdrawn demeanor falsely creates the impression that nothing is wrong.

Thus, neither the passive nor the provocative socially vulnerable child can win. Schools may not intervene unless there is overwhelming and uncontested data to support the bullying. And given the problems inherent in defining and detecting bullying behaviors, as well as the tendency to blame the victim, hard evidence rarely emerges. For this reason, it's time to start paying more attention to the characteristics of the bully and her role in the bullying process.

What About the Bully?

As we mentioned previously, most bullies are neither unpopular nor have low self-esteem. Generally speaking, research (Olweus 1993) suggests that bullies have a higher level of need for control, power, and dominance than their victims do. Bullies are also more likely to exhibit angry, hostile, or impulsive behaviors, and a lack of caring and empathy toward their victims.

Boys who bully are more likely to be physically stronger and aggressive toward their weaker victims, and they tend to feel good about their aggressive behavior as a means of accomplishing goals, achieving status, or prestige. Girls who bully, on the other hand, are more likely to relish being the center of attention and use less-direct relational bullying tactics to exclude and isolate their less socially sophisticated victims.

Perhaps the most striking characteristic of bullies, irrespective of gender, is an attitude of contempt. Barbara Coloroso, in her book *The Bully, the Bullied, and the Bystander*, says that contempt is about having a total disregard for someone and seeing them as possessing no value. She says that contempt is associated with "a sense of entitlement, intolerance toward differences, and a liberty to exclude" (Coloroso 2003, 21). Entitlement is the bully's feeling that she has the right to harass and abuse her victim. Someone who is intolerant of differences sees being different as a bad thing. Socially vulnerable children, especially provocative victims, often stand out and are viewed as different; Ira, for example, is repeatedly referred to as "different" in sarcastic, hostile ways by his classmates. Naturally, when a bully views another child as being different in a negative way and having no value, she will take it upon herself to help isolate and exclude the inferior victim.

Family Matters

Now that we've discussed the various roles that bullies and victims play and the types of bullying behavior, you now may be wondering how a child could develop such a contemptuous attitude and become a bully. Indeed, attitude is everything. Both the socially vulnerable child and bully are likely to have negative attitudes. The socially vulnerable child's negativity reflects her own personal struggles, frustrations, and peer victimization. As a result, she experiences anxiety, depression, social withdrawal, or all three. The bully's negative attitude on the other hand, given that she is neither unpopular nor suffering from low self-esteem, more likely reflects the raw emotion of her family environment. Such emotion is typically expressed in the form of anger, hostility, and cynicism toward others. Scapegoating is common both within and outside the family (Olweus 1993; Patterson 1982). Thus, it's not surprising that family environments can serve as breeding grounds for contempt in children.

Ira recently befriended another child at school, but he was devastated to learn that the child's mother had refused to let Ira play with him. She actually told her son (who then told Ira), "Stay away from that troubled child; he'll just embarrass you." The mother had never even met Ira, but nonetheless she had developed contempt for him, which she was attempting to pass on to her son.

In addition to contempt, families of aggressive children often experience strong levels of conflict and aggressive behavior. Parent-child relationships in these families are characterized as overly controlling, and punitive methods of punishment (physical and/or overly emotional) are frequently utilized. The child learns through parental models that aggressive and defiant behaviors are effective ways of controlling people and getting what they want.

It's important to keep in mind that family conflict alone is not terribly predictive of bullying behaviors in children. Rather, the combination of high levels of family conflict and low levels of parental support make bullying behavior more likely. Families of aggressive children often lack warmth, empathy, and guidance. Supervision and healthy limit setting also tend to be lenient (Olweus 1993).

Of course, not every child with a negative attitude, family conflict, and lack of support will become a bully. It also depends on the child's temperament. For instance, a child with a high-intensity temperament is more likely to externalize (act out) the harsh circumstances of her family environment than is a child with a low-key, passive temperament. And, even when all the factors are ripe for the development of bullying, a loving, secure relationship with the primary caregiver greatly reduces the child's risk for engaging in antisocial behaviors.

As you can see, the development of bullying behaviors involves a complex interplay of factors. Understanding bullying is one thing.

Protecting your child is another thing, and, of course, one of greater importance.

The Reality of Reporting and Stopping Bullying

Children who are bullied are often reluctant to report their concerns to adults for a number of reasons. For instance, Jeremy keeps it to himself because of his indifference to his peers. Tracey, as much as she wants to fit in, doesn't know how to ask for help and becomes more withdrawn. Ralph and Ira make some effort to inform adults; however, educators and school personnel minimize or dismiss their concerns and continue to blame the victims. Ralph retreats to avoid rejection; Ira does so as well since he fears getting into trouble and being branded a tattletale. Clearly, a scarcity of reports of bullying does not mean that bullying is not occurring.

Even when educators and school personnel do try to intervene, their efforts are often ineffective and result in increased bullying. As a first step, educators and school personnel may try character education or peer mediation. Character education does not work; socially savvy bullies know how to present themselves as having good character and often pose as model students. Peer mediation efforts are no better. Remember, bullying is about an unevenness of power. In a situation where the bully and victim are in the same room, not only will the socially savvy bully know what to say, but she will win over the adult and intimidate her victim (with nonverbal body language) all at the same time. She will also blame the victim for this unnecessary confrontation, and in the future she will become more creative in her efforts to harass without being seen.

What about having school personnel contact the parent of the bully (which, by the way, rarely happens)? The bully will change her story, and, of course, her henchmen will support her. Who is the parent going to believe? Her smart, popular child who can do no wrong or that "troubled" socially vulnerable victim? If anything, the parent of the bully will tell her child to stay away from the victim, assuming it was the victim's fault.

If your child is being bullied, you likely know that the conspiracy runs deep. Our bullying climate will only change when adults change their attitudes about the signs, symptoms, and impact that bullying is having on our youth. Bullying identification, intervention, and prevention requires a systemic approach that involves children (victims, bullies, bystanders, and defenders), parents, teachers, educators, and school personnel working together. But for now, it begins with you: you can start the process by identifying some early signs that may indicate that your child is a victim of bullying (Coloroso 2003; Sprague and Walker 2005). If your child is being bullied she may experience any of the following:

- Lost or damaged belongings (clothes, electronics, or school books)

- Injuries (with stories that don't ring true)

- Social withdrawal, loneliness, or isolation

- Sadness, sulking, or sudden crying spells

- Annoyed, pessimistic, negative, overly critical manner or moods

- Anger, rage, or explosive outbursts

- Loss of interest in school, sports, or community activities

- Separation anxiety; school avoidance or refusal

- Somatic complaints, worry, or anxiety

- Sleeping problems (difficulty falling asleep or staying asleep; taking frequent naps)

- Hitting, swearing, or lashing out (especially with younger siblings)

- Items missing from your home (such as money or jewelry)

- Appetite changes

- Bladder problems (including reluctance to use bathroom at school or other places)

Summary

In this chapter, you've learned about the difference between teasing and bullying, the different types of bullying behaviors, the dynamics of bullying, and some of the signs that your child may be a victim of bullying. In chapter 5, we will set the stage for your child to develop greater social competence and improved peer relations. This can be accomplished by first helping to manage her natural shyness, social anxiety, and/or withdrawal. In chapters 6, 7, and 8, we will then address more pronounced social problems stemming from key types of social vulnerability and the experience of being bullied.

Recommended Resources

Bierman, K. L. 2004. *Peer Rejection*. New York: Guilford Press.

Coloroso, B. 2003. *The Bully, the Bullied, and the Bystander*. New York: Harper Resource.

Garbarino, J., and E. deLara. 2002. *And Words Can Hurt Forever*. New York: Free Press.

5

What to Do When Your Child Is Shy or Socially Anxious

I let Isabelle stay with me for a few minutes at the party and then she went over and played with two friends. I never thought that would happen.

—Karen

Chapter Objectives

In this chapter you will learn the following:

- Guiding principles to help your child become more socially secure

- How to plan a step-by-step program to address your child's unique social needs

- Specific coping strategies for managing the key forms of shyness or social anxiety in children and adolescents

Get Ready

In this chapter we discuss guiding principles for each type of shyness or social anxiety, which will help you maximize your child's growth toward becoming more assertive, confident, calm, or motivated. Each principle builds on the next, regardless of your child's specific form of shyness or social anxiety.

So, are you ready? It's time to put it all together to help your child overcome his shyness or social anxiety. As you prepare, remember that every child progresses at his own pace. Gradually build your child's confidence by helping him take small steps. We'll guide you every step of the way using our real-life examples, looking at four children's step-by-step plans for helping them become more comfortable and confident in social situations. Let's begin with Karen and Liam's plan for helping Isabelle become more socially involved.

Isabelle: Warming Up

As you may remember from chapter 1, Isabelle is a sweet, sensitive, and shy seven-year-old girl. She is very comfortable playing with her dad or best friend, Lilly, around her neighborhood. However, when two or more children are involved, Isabelle becomes overwhelmed. Her mom, Karen, explains that Isabelle's demeanor quickly changes from playful and happy to frightened and tearful. Sometimes, with encouragement, Isabelle will approach another child, but she immediately withdraws when someone else joins in. Isabelle is also fearful of new situations and activities such as attending birthday parties and family gatherings. She rarely participates during school and extracurricular activities. If your child is like Isabelle, you likely have several goals in mind. Karen and Liam want Isabelle to be able to do the following:

- Try new activities without too much fuss

- Stay in social situations even when she becomes anxious

- Participate more fully in social activities

- Take initiative with other children

In order to best help Isabelle, Karen and Liam have broken down their broad goals into specific, concrete, and manageable steps called "exposures," which are real-life situations that help children master their fears by confronting and feeling them (Eisen and Engler 2006). Isabelle has to learn that it's okay for her to feel nervous during social confrontations. She has to give herself a chance to stay in the situation, accept the anxiety, calm down, and realize some social success. When Isabelle avoids or withdraws from the situations she fears, all she remembers is how scared she was, and it is this uncomfortable feeling that both sustains her anxiety and encourages her to avoid similar situations in the future. Let's take a look at Isabelle's list of social goals, which could serve as possible exposures for her.

Isabelle's Social Goals

Neighborhood Activities

- Invite a friend over (at school or on the phone)

- Visit a friend (planned playdate or spontaneous visit)

- Play with two children at once (her house or friend's house)

Social Events

- Attend and participate at birthday parties

- Attend and participate in meals at restaurants

- Attend and participate at family gatherings

School Situations

- Answer questions in class when called upon

- Raise hand to volunteer to answer a question in class

- Play with two children at once

- Join a group

- Ask her teacher for help

Extracurricular Activities

- Attend and participate at soccer practice and games

- Attend and participate in new activity (swimming lessons)

Now, you're ready to devise a similar list of social goals for your child. First, think of all the specific places and social situations in which you would like your child to be able to be more actively involved. Then, take each situation and break it down into a series of small steps. Be sure to have him first observe (if necessary), then attend, and ultimately participate in each situation to an increasing degree.

If your child is like Isabelle, you want to build on your child's present level of socialization. Isabelle is playing with Lilly, going to school, and ultimately attending social and extracurricular activities—she is trying and wants to participate more fully. If Isabelle were to dwell on her anxiety and lack of participation, this could easily lead to social withdrawal. Let's review three fundamental, guiding principles that will help your child build on his socialization successes and overcome his shyness or social anxiety: (1) be proactive, (2) be patient, and (3) be prepared.

Be Proactive

Being proactive means thinking ahead and planning how to best facilitate positive social interactions for your child. It requires accepting and respecting your child's shyness. It means always taking into account his tendency to warm up slowly, stay by himself, and observe before participating.

If your child is like Isabelle, participation in any new activity or social event will require much planning on your part. Given the hectic pace of modern family life, it can be very difficult to put in the time to help each social situation go smoothly. Because of time constraints, you may really want your child to just blend in and cope naturally. When he doesn't, you may find yourself expecting or hoping that he will adapt better the next time. But in your heart, however, you know that without prior planning, this is unlikely.

Sometimes, your own personality or parenting style can affect how you view your child's shyness. Karen, an outgoing and a self-proclaimed extrovert, had difficulty accepting Isabelle's shyness and went overboard in her efforts to push Isabelle to participate. When Karen forced participation, however, Isabelle shut down. Liam, on the other hand, was quiet and sensitive by nature. He understood Isabelle's plight and was careful not to upset her. But Liam also didn't challenge his daughter. An approach somewhere in the middle may be more effective in helping children overcome shyness. In using this approach, you'll need to follow our next principle, *be patient*.

Be Patient

It is one thing to understand and accept your child's shyness, but it's quite another to remain calm when he freezes or melts down in social situations. Of course we feel frustrated and embarrassed, possibly thinking that he is behaving this way on purpose. Accepting your child's shyness makes it less likely that you will view his behavior as intentional or manipulative, but this doesn't necessarily make your child's intense reactions any easier to manage. And, of course, as your patience decreases his behavior is likely to worsen. What's a parent to do? Unfortunately, the common reaction is to let the child leave the situation or event prematurely.

When this happens, you cannot help but feel resentment toward your child. But remember, if your child is like Isabelle, he likely struggles with cognitive distortions (see chapter 1). One of these is person-alization, which means that he will view the unpleasant outcome (the fact that he left the situation prematurely) as entirely his fault. He may be so hard on himself that reprimands or punishment are of little value and only make the situation worse.

The other cognitive distortion he may experience is all-or-nothing thinking. Leaving early encourages your child to think that because he couldn't stay for the entire event, the whole situation was a failure. Evaluating outcomes this way can lead to greater avoidance and social withdrawal. Thus, in order to limit avoidance and withdrawal, your child has to remain in the situation even when he thinks he cannot. He needs to stay there even if he is inconsolable and drawing too much attention to himself. This is where patience comes in.

Being patient means expecting that your child will become overwhelmed; cry, freeze, or have a tantrum; or refuse to attend or participate (becoming oppositional or inconsolable). As you know, being patient on any regular basis is no easy task. This leads us to our next guiding principle, *be prepared*.

Be Prepared

When planning a dinner party or your next family vacation, preparation equals success. Would you invite your friends over for dinner without planning a menu, shopping, and cooking? Would you travel to a popular location without making reservations? Of course not. Let's see how being prepared can make it easier for you to help your child become more socially active and less fearful.

Try new activities. Helping your child try a range of new social events such as birthday parties, family gatherings, and extracurricular activities is a key element in his progress. The following paragraphs give several tips that will help him feel more comfortable trying new activities.

> *Educate your child.* Help him understand his shy, slow-to-warm-up temperament. Let him know that it's okay if he first observes and then takes some time before participating. Help him feel secure knowing that there is no pressure to join quickly. If necessary, agree to stay close by, as long as he doesn't cling.

You can also point out other children who may also be reluctant to participate. This will help him feel less alone, so he won't feel quite so negative toward himself.

Emphasize attendance. Children like Isabelle may not be able to visualize themselves participating in a new activity and thus will shut down. Do not promise that he won't have to participate. Rather, simply leave it up to him. Doing so will help your child feel more in control. Once he warms up he is more likely to take bolder steps.

Emphasize small successes. If your child has an all-or-nothing thinking style, any disappointment that you express, either verbally or nonverbally (such as sighing), will be interpreted by your child as failure. If you can find something to praise, even small successes or simple steps in the right direction, this will help build momentum so that he can take on greater challenges.

Do your homework. When a new social event like a birthday party or a restaurant dinner is coming up, let your child check out the location beforehand. Help him become acclimated to the surroundings. Let him see where he will be sitting and discuss what he will be doing. Emphasize the exciting features of the event (for instance, his best friend will be there, his favorite food will be served, or he'll get to do a favorite activity). Take note of any aspects of the location that might cause your child to become overwhelmed (the music is too loud, for example), and think about how you can minimize its impact. Before signing him up for a team or other group activity, you might consider enrolling him in private lessons as a first step.

Consider contingent rewards. A reward is not the same as a bribe. Granting a privilege (such as watching television) in order to stop a child's acting-out behaviors is an example of a bribe. This is not an effective technique. In fact, such an arrangement may actually increase the likelihood that the child will choose the inappropriate behavior again. A reward, however, is a positive consequence of a desired behavior, and it will increase the likelihood that the child will choose the positive behavior again. A reward may help your child work hard to overcome his shyness or social anxiety. In fact, a small contingent reward, planned in advance, can make all the difference in determining whether your child will attempt new social situations   .

You don't need to spend a great deal of money. Rewards can consist of small, inexpensive items (for instance, sports or trading cards, stickers, and hair accessories) and/or social/home activities (for instance, being allowed to rent a video, stay up later than usual, or use the television or computer), along with plenty of praise. Rewards should be given after the successful completion of an exposure, meaning simply getting through the exposure, even if he feels nervous or uncomfortable. Social anxiety is both expected and allowed while the child is working through the exposure. Once your child successfully completes an exposure a few times, you can now expect him to handle similar situations without a reward. He then moves on to the next situation on his list of social goals, which will likely be a bit more challenging, and you can give a reward for completion of that exposure. Remember not to give your child the reward until after he has gotten through the situation successfully.

Stay in social situations even when anxious.   Getting your child to attend social gatherings is one thing. Helping him stay there when he becomes anxious is quite another. You can use the following strategies to help your child cope during anxiety-provoking social events. Prior to using them during exposures, have your child practice these strategies until he learns them well.

Use deep-breathing exercises.   Deep breathing is one of the easiest and most effective ways for children to calm down when they're under stress. Having a way to calm down is especially important, since social anxiety often escalates quickly. You can help your child relax by having him follow our four-step sequence (Eisen and Engler 2006):

1. Ask your child to breathe in. Be sure he inhales slowly and deeply through his nose. Count out loud (to three) so he can follow your pace.

2. Ask him to breathe out. Be sure your child blows out through his mouth slowly and gently. Count out loud so he can follow your pace.

3. Help him practice the breathing exercises until he can breathe in and out on cue.

4. Help him master the breathing exercises in low-anxiety situations before moving onto more-anxiety-provoking exposures.

Use deep muscle relaxation. Deep muscle relaxation involves first tensing different muscle groups and then relaxing them. The idea is that it's impossible to be both tense and relaxed all at once, and if your child can learn to differentiate between the two, he will be better able to bring on relaxation, which will make him feel more in control. These exercises (adapted from Ollendick and Cerny 1981) are also an excellent way to help your child cope with anger. You can help your child relax by having him follow our four-step sequence:

1. Demonstrate for your child how to tense and relax each of the muscle groups (see below). Have him tense for three seconds, and relax for three seconds. When he relaxes, help him let go as completely as possible. You want him to learn to experience a sense of calm and relief after each exercise. Below you will find a list of the muscle groups that your child will be tensing and relaxing. You can have your child practice them all or simply use those groups that he is most sensitive to (like the stomach). Each muscle group has several possible exercises. Try them out with your child to determine his preferences.

a. Hands and Arms

- Squeeze your fists.

- Show me your muscles (biceps).

- Stretch your arms above your head.

b. Shoulders

- Tense your shoulders.

- Lift your shoulders up to your ears.

- Stretch your arms out to your side.

c. Mouth

- Press your lips together.

- Open your mouth wide.

d. Stomach

- Hold your stomach in.

- Make your middle as thin as you can.

- Tighten up your stomach.

e. Head

- Arch your eyebrows.

- Tighten your nose.

- Make wrinkles on your forehead.

f. Legs and Feet

- Push your feet down (on the floor).

- Stretch your legs.

- Curl your toes (upward or downward).

2. Help him practice until he can perform the exercises on cue when you ask him to.

3. Help him use the exercises when faced with social situations that make him anxious; they may help him avoid crying, freezing, or having a tantrum.

4. Help him master the exercises in low-pressure situations before moving onto more-anxiety-provoking exposures.

Use distraction. An important part of being prepared is anticipating how your child is likely to respond to any given social situation. In situations where relaxation exercises might not work, you can also consider using distraction. With this approach, you'll come prepared with activities (such as books, magazines, and small toys) to keep him busy. Distraction can help your child stay in challenging situations by keeping him temporarily preoccupied. It's important to remember, however, that distraction is another form of avoidance behavior. Distraction minimizes your child's chance to feel the fear and learn that he can survive it, which is needed for him to overcome his social anxiety. Thus, we recommend that you allow your child to be distracted only as a first step in getting through a difficult exposure. Then have your child complete the same exposure without allowing him to be distracted. This will be more difficult, but it is essential for your child to be able to fully conquer his anxiety.

Shape your child's behavior. The idea behind shaping is that you give your child lots of positive attention (praise) for behaving appropriately and minimal attention for inappropriate or fearful behaviors. At this point, your child is likely receiving too much attention (positive or negative) for socially anxious behaviors, and this ultimately helps to sustain his anxiety. Instead, try turning it around, and give him attention for his efforts to cope with shyness and/or social anxiety. You can shape your child's behavior by following our three-step sequence (Eisen and Engler 2006):

1. Pay attention to and praise your child's efforts to cope with shyness or social anxiety.

2. Let your child know that you understand he is scared, without giving attention to his fearful behaviors. For example, if your child has a tantrum and insists on leaving a birthday party, you could say something like "I know you're afraid to stay here, but I cannot talk about it until you are calm." Be sure to use a calm, neutral voice.

3. Do your best to ignore your child's fearful or inappropriate behaviors, keeping in mind that getting anxious is a natural part of the process. Expect it. Be prepared for it. Do help him calm down by encouraging him to use breathing and relaxation as well as distraction. Emphasize his efforts to become calm rather than focusing on the tantrum or panic that preceded it.

Consider spontaneous rewards. If all else fails, and your child remains inconsolable, a spontaneous reward can help him "unlock" and be able to focus on using the coping strategies. Examples include trading cards, stickers, or small toys that you can keep in a purse, pocket, or wallet and bring out if needed. Once again, give the reward only after your child has calmed down and then praise his ability to do so.

Participate more fully in social activities. Once your child is able to attend and stay in social situations, you can then focus your efforts on helping him to participate more fully. If your child is like Isabelle, joining a group and playing with two other children at the same time are likely your key concerns. As you know, Isabelle is perfectly happy to socialize with one child, but she will fall apart when two other children are involved. She simply doesn't know what to say or do and quickly becomes overwhelmed. Teaching and practicing some of the following basic social skills exercises with your child can help build his confidence so he can more easily deal with overwhelming situations.

Use nonverbal forms of participation. As a first step, help your child join unstructured group play situations where conversation is kept to a minimum. Examples include playing a noncompetitive game with children in the neighborhood, joining a group of kids on the jungle gym at recess, or attending an activity-oriented party. Explain that participation does not always have to involve conversation and that tagging along is perfectly acceptable. Teach your child the importance of showing an interest through consistent eye contact, nodding, smiling, and laughing appropriately. Model this skill for your child with one other family member. Show him how the family member responds when you listen attentively and when you lose interest. Help your child practice the skill, and ask family members to emphasize his efforts, giving him constructive feedback and plenty of praise.

Practice in real-life, familiar, structured situations. As you recall, Isabelle is perfectly comfortable interacting with her best friend, Lilly, in the neighborhood. For this reason, Karen encouraged Isabelle to practice her listening skills with Lilly. As a first step, Karen prompted Isabelle to ask Lilly a question such as "Did you like the movie?" You may decide to do the same with your child. In a situation that's comfortable to your child, use positive nonverbal body language (a smile, wink, or thumbs-up) to guide your child's interactions. With repeated practice using best friends and family members, your child will soon feel like a "master listener." You can then add another peer to the equation.

Develop a terrific trio. Children like Isabelle may be strong willed *and* terrified of interacting with two other children, both at the same time. For this reason, take special care in helping your child find a third friend to complete the trio and build his social confidence. An ideal third member is sociable enough to keep conversations going but also even tempered enough to tolerate your child's sudden anxiety, frustration, or withdrawal. Consider children in your neighborhood, relatives, or family friends. Your goal is to help your child initially tolerate and ultimately accept another member of his small group. Continue to emphasize nonverbal participation and staying with the group. Encourage deep breathing and muscle relaxation, and use contingent or spontaneous rewards as needed. Keep practicing until your child is comfortable attending and listening to others in small groups and does not feel pressure to speak.

Practice conversational skills. You can continue to help your child show an interest in others by asking others questions about themselves in addition to communicating nonverbally. Role-play and practice with your child, showing him how you keep conversations going, by continuing to ask him questions about himself. After repeated practice, switch roles and have your child ask you questions to keep the conversation going. Praise his efforts and compliment his newly developed conversational skills. Help him develop a list of favorite topics that he can discuss with other children. Then have him practice first with one child and then with small groups while you prompt him with nonverbal feedback. Use friends, relatives, and low-key peers in comfortable, safe settings, like your neighborhood or other favorite places. As your child becomes increasingly confident, prompt him less and less and eventually remove yourself from these interactions. These exercises will build your child's confidence in his ability to join groups.

Take initiative with other children. Accepting another child into an already existing duo is one thing. Joining an already established group, of course, is much more difficult. Before you help your child accomplish this goal, help him first take initiative in small ways. For example, at home, encourage him to call a friend for a playdate. If necessary, break it down into small exposures, such as first making the call yourself, then simply asking your child to say hello, and finally staying close by while he talks on the phone. After he has practiced this several times, encourage your child to take more responsibility for initiating the playdate. Leaving messages on answering machines counts. (Even adults experience anxiety about leaving messages in these kinds of "pressured" situations.)

At school, develop a monitoring system (with home-based rewards) with your child's teacher for keeping track of how often your child says hello to other children, asks for help, raises his hand, or joins a group. When you're out in the community, encourage your child to order his own food at a restaurant or ask for help with locating a toy at a store. Don't allow your child to hide behind you, but do accept any effort on his part such as a whisper or nonverbal gesture, especially at first. Over time, these steps will help your child become more socially confident in these situations.

When your child is ready, help him join groups of kids he already knows in comfortable, safe settings like your neighborhood park, a family party, or the town pool. In these scenarios, help your child join the group by encouraging him to smile and use other nonverbal forms of participation. Emphasize staying with the group for brief intervals. Encourage him to use his breathing and relaxation exercises, and be prepared to use both contingent and spontaneous rewards to help him as needed. Help him practice asking questions, seeking information, and offering compliments. As your child's confidence builds, he can follow this sequence as he attempts to join groups of kids he doesn't know as well. Role-play and practice with family members how he might ask to join a group and how he could handle less-than-receptive responses. Continue to create new social scenarios so that you can help him practice, prepare (remind himself what to do), and perfect (master) his skills. With patience and persistence, watch your child's slow-to-warm-up style blossom into newly developed social confidence.

Next, we address our "self-conscious" type with our real-life story of Stephen and his parents, Walter and Lorraine.

Stephen: Becoming More Confident

Stephen, as you will recall, is a bright, pleasant, and gentle ten-year-old boy. He does well in school, is an excellent athlete, and is well liked by his peers and teachers. But Stephen worries about making mistakes, wants everyone to like him, and is extremely self-critical.

He naturally succeeds in his schoolwork and sports without much effort, yet he holds back and shuts down if he makes a single mistake. Walter and Lorraine remark that Stephen is like two different people. At home, he is comfortable and confident and has a good sense of humor. Yet away from home he is riddled with self-doubt and low self-esteem.

If your child is like Stephen, you likely have several goals in mind. Walter and Lorraine want Stephen to be able to do the following:

■ Become less concerned about making mistakes

■ Become more confident when playing sports

Like Karen and Liam did with Isabelle, Walter and Lorraine broke down their broad goals into specific, concrete, and manageable steps. Let's take a look at Stephen's list of goals, which could serve as a list of possible exposures.

Stephen's "Take Charge" List

School and Social Situations

■ Answer questions in class

■ Raise hand

■ Ask others for help

■ Handle getting into trouble

Sports

■ Play with confidence during practice

■ Play with confidence during competitions (with family not present)

■ Play with confidence during competitions (with family present)

You may wish to devise a similar list for your child. Think of all the specific places and social situations in which you would like him to be able to take charge more effectively. You may have to break down some situations into several smaller steps.

Unlike Isabelle, Stephen is not really avoiding social situations. He regularly participates both at school and in sports, but he doesn't try his hardest, out of fear of making mistakes and/or losing the approval of his parents, teachers, and coaches. Still, our first three guiding principles (be proactive, be patient, and be prepared) and their strategies also apply to Stephen. But, more important, Stephen can also benefit from a fourth guiding principle. He has to learn to *think more realistically about his expectations* for success and develop a better understanding of his strong need for approval. And this begins with taking a closer look at his parents' expectations.

Be Mindful of Your Expectations

If your child is like Stephen, you may wonder why he is so loved by others yet feels so completely inadequate. This reaction is the hallmark of a "self-conscious" child. Why is Stephen this way? First, let's take a closer look at Walter and Lorraine's expectations of their son.

Walter is very intense and competitive. On one hand, he fully appreciates his son's superior intelligence and athletic ability. On the other hand, he underestimates the extent of Stephen's self-consciousness. Walter knows what Stephen is capable of, believes he should be performing better, and gets very frustrated when he sees him holding back. Walter intends his occasionally critical feedback to be a force that will help Stephen become more successful. What he doesn't fully appreciate, however, is that he cannot force his son to develop a "killer instinct."

Lorraine is more supportive, and at times she is overprotective. She knows how hard Stephen is on himself and that he doesn't need others to criticize him. For this reason, she takes the other extreme, constantly praising Stephen regarding everything he does. What Lorraine doesn't fully appreciate, however, is that frequent, nonspecific parental praise quickly loses its value and will not be enough to help Stephen develop positive self-esteem.

So, we have two very different parenting styles, both carried out with the best of intentions. One teaches Stephen to emphasize the negative, and the other plays down Stephen's concerns, and, by doing so, may contribute to his feeling of guilt about making mistakes. Let's look at how Walter and Lorraine's expectations feed into Stephen's self-consciousness.

As you recall from chapter 1, Stephen struggles with two key cognitive distortions: all-or-nothing thinking, which causes him to see a single mistake as evidence of failure, and a negative filter, which makes him see only the negative side of a situation. In Stephen's case, it's not that he cannot tolerate making mistakes. Rather, to him, making mistakes means a loss of approval from important others. Because of Stephen's negative filter, even when he appears successful (for instance, when he gets three hits during a baseball game), he still dwells on the negative (his dad's nonverbal expression of disappointment in response to Stephen's single strikeout).

Deep down, Stephen cannot feel good about himself unless he has the complete approval of important others in his life. And, as you can imagine, it's rare for any person to get the complete approval of everyone in his life. Stephen has always been self-conscious, and he will continue to be vulnerable as long as he needs the unconditional positive approval of others.

If your child is like Stephen, you'll want to be mindful of how your expectations could be affecting his behavior. You'll also need to help him learn to evaluate situations in constructive ways, and most important, learn the value of self-praise. Let's see how we can help Walter and Lorraine accomplish their goals for Stephen.

Become less concerned about making mistakes.

Identify automatic thoughts. The first step toward helping your self-conscious child become less self-critical is to identify his automatic (unrealistic) thoughts. Automatic thoughts and questions are our brains' way of telling us that we're anxious. Without warning, these thoughts pop into our heads, make us feel uncomfortable, and tell us that unfortunate events or outcomes are inevitable. Let's take a look at some of Stephen's self-conscious automatic thoughts, or questions, and examine how he feels when he thinks this way.

Thought: [*at school*] What if I make a mistake? What if I get into trouble?

Feeling: No one will like me anymore.

Thought: [*at baseball game*] What if we lose the game? What if I let my dad [or coach, or team] down?

Feeling: It's all my fault.

As you can see, Stephen's self-worth is directly related to his performance or even his entire team's performance. The problem, however, is that there is no truth to his automatic questions, and, if left unchallenged, these questions will continue to diminish his self-esteem. This leads us to our next step.

Challenge automatic thoughts. You can help your child challenge his automatic thoughts by asking him evidence-based questions that are drawn from commonly used cognitive therapy techniques (Beck 1995; Friedberg and McClure 2002).

- "How often do you make mistakes (at school or in sports)?"

- When was the last time you made a mistake?"

You can also use follow-up questions to help your child see the situation more accurately. For example, if he says he makes mistakes at school "all the time," you can respond by asking, "How many times have you received a poor grade on a test or report card?"

Your goal is to help your child realize that the things he's worrying about have little or no chance of occurring. Refrain from minimizing his fears by saying, for instance, "Everything will be okay" or "Don't worry about it." This kind of reassurance doesn't allow him to feel the fear nor learn how to challenge his automatic thoughts on his own.

Challenge feelings. Once your child realizes the lack of truth in his automatic thoughts, he will be ready to challenge his feelings associated with these thoughts or situations. You can ask him any of the following questions:

- "Did anyone get mad at you for striking out?"

- "If so, who was it and how could you tell?"

- "Did you lose any friends?"

Your goal is to help your child develop an understanding of the broader context ("the big picture"), so that he can more realistically evaluate his thoughts and feelings. By doing so, you will help him understand that even if he makes a mistake, nothing terrible is likely to result. Encourage him to be as specific as possible when he answers these questions. Feelings, no matter how subtle, often do not reflect reality and may become overgeneralized.

Diminish personal responsibility for group success or failure. Being self-conscious comes in part from (1) accepting all the blame for failure and (2) overlooking one's contribution toward group success. Like many self-conscious children, Stephen feared being the last one to bat and then striking out. This had never occurred, but if it were to happen Stephen would undoubtedly feel that he had blown the game no matter what his previous performance had been. The idea is to help your child understand the actual role he plays in determining group outcomes. You can ask him any of the following questions:

- "Were you completely responsible for winning the game?"

- "Did you lose the game all by yourself?"

- "If you feel that way, what exactly did you do that caused that to happen?"

Do your best to guide your child's answers so they reflect his efforts rather than his performance. This means giving him minimal attention when he becomes overexcited about winning or extremely upset about losing, and lots of attention when he says that he did his best.

Accept less-than-perfect outcomes.   With repeated practice in real-life social or performance situations, your child will worry less about making mistakes and feel less responsible for negative outcomes. Ultimately, however, you will also want to work toward helping your child accept less-than-perfect outcomes. This is no easy task given that your child is naturally self-conscious. Making it even more difficult is the fact that we live in a perfectionistic world—even as you keep your own expectations for him in check, your child's teachers, coaches, and peers may not. To help him deal with his own mistakes, prompt your child to say any of the following when he's evaluating a performance-based outcome:

- "As long as I try my best, I don't have to be perfect."

- "It's okay if I make mistakes; everyone does."

Remember, your child is not used to thinking this way. At first, it may feel fake and he may resist saying these statements. Over time, however, with your support and guidance, he will become a true believer.

Encourage healthy (constructive) self-evaluations.   Once your child can accept less-than-perfect outcomes, he will be ready to evaluate situations in healthier ways. "Healthy" does not simply mean positive thinking (being positive—for instance, saying "I played a great game!"—may not be realistic or accurate). Healthy thinking (Kendall 1992) allows a person to examine situations constructively, emphasize effort and small successes, and come up with a plan of action when needed. Healthy thinking will help your child preserve his self-esteem even when his performance is not ideal. So when Stephen sulks about striking out, saying "I blew the game," Walter and Lorraine can prompt him to say the following:

- "I did my best and I cannot do better than that." (effort)

- "I did get three hits." (small successes)

- "If I'm disappointed, I'll try harder the next time and get extra batting practice." (action plan)

Remember, your child is used to evaluating outcomes in negative ways. Expect such negativity, especially at first, and say, "Can you think about yourself in a better way?" Guide him to emphasize his efforts, small successes, and what he will do differently the next time. Most important, help him get into the habit of saying "I'm proud of myself." Make your praise contingent upon his healthy self-evaluations rather than his performance.

Become more confident when playing sports. Now that your child is becoming less self-conscious in his way of thinking, practicing in real-life social or performance situations will ultimately boost his self-confidence. For Stephen, baseball games with his family present were the true test. It was easiest for him to feel good about his performance when his family was absent or out of sight, and hardest when he could see his dad watching. Walter and Lorraine arranged the following sequence of exposures:

1. The family doesn't attend the game or remains out of sight. (Encourage, support, and praise your child's healthy self-evaluations.)

2. One very encouraging family member attends. (Repeat the process. Remember to avoid palliative reassurances such as "It'll be all right.")

3. Several family members (some encouraging, some less so) are present. Repeat the process. Be sure to monitor your nonverbal feedback.

4. Repeat as needed in other relevant sports competitions. Make your praise contingent upon your child's healthy self-evaluations.

If you implement a similar strategy with your child, over time, like Stephen, he will learn to appreciate his accomplishments, develop more positive self-esteem, become less dependent on your feedback, and grow stronger emotionally.

Now, let's take a look at our "social or performance anxiety" type in our real-life story of Beth, and her parents, Alan and Amy.

Beth: Doing Her Best

Beth is a quiet, intense, and responsible eleven-year-old girl. She does well in school, is popular with her peers, and is a gifted tennis player. Yet Beth is struggling when it comes to playing competitive tennis. Before each match she feels physically sick and fears vomiting. These uncomfortable physical feelings are related to her strong fear of failure. Beth's parents, Alan and Amy, are trying to understand why she feels this way. Neither is overly critical, nor does either of them put any pressure on Beth to excel. In fact, both parents have always expressed contentment with Beth's efforts at school and in sports. If anything, they both feel upset that Beth gets this way. Uncertain of how to proceed, they are considering allowing Beth to take a break from competitive tennis play.

If your child is like Beth, you likely have several goals in mind. Alan and Amy want Beth to be able to do the following:

- Understand and tolerate uncomfortable physical feelings

- Develop a healthy attitude about playing competitive sports

Let's take a look at Beth's list of goals for helping her "be cool" in stressful situations, which could serve as possible exposures.

Beth's "Be Cool" List

Think About Competitive Tennis Play

■ Talk about competitive tennis (general)

■ Watch competitive tennis (television)

■ Talk about forthcoming tennis matches

Observe Competitive Tennis Play

■ Attend adult competitive tennis tournament

■ Observe peers playing competitive tennis (middle school tennis team)

Play Competitive Tennis

■ Play in less-competitive tournament with same-age peers

■ Play in middle school team match

Like Stephen, Beth also experiences social and performance anxiety. For this reason, the cognitive therapy strategies designed to help Stephen become more confident will also help Beth stay calm. But Beth is not simply worried about making mistakes or losing the approval of others. She is also terrified about the possibility of failing (losing) and/or vomiting. To help her experience and learn to tolerate these unpleasant thoughts and physical feelings, her "be cool" list contains situations that will trigger the problem thoughts and feelings. In the process, Beth is going to need lots of help with gaining control of her automatic thoughts. In addition, she will also benefit from the deep breathing and muscle relaxation exercises given in the section about Isabelle. But, given that Beth is older and more sophisticated in her cognitive processes, she will also require a greater understanding of what is happening to her body. This brings us to our next principle, *be consistent*.

Be Consistent

Alan and Amy are ambivalent about putting pressure on Beth to play competitive tennis. After all, she works hard and does so well in all other areas of her life. What would be the harm in letting her avoid situations where she feels overwhelmed? If they followed this approach, Beth would be completely bored and unchallenged in her tennis game. More important, what message would Alan and Amy be giving Beth if they let her take a break from competitive play because of her social and performance anxiety? It would be better for them to be consistent in their insistence that she face her fears. They can do this by gradually exposing Beth to anxiety-provoking situations without overwhelming her, so that she can gain control of her anxious thoughts and bodily feelings. Remember, thinking about a dreaded social or performance situation is nearly always worse than experiencing the actual outcome—every time Beth avoids a performance-based situation, in her mind she has avoided the humiliation of vomiting and losing the match. Confronting and feeling the fear on a regular basis, even through small steps, is the only way to overcome anxiety.

Like Stephen, Beth also struggles with cognitive distortions, but she engages in catastrophic thinking. She automatically assumes that the worst possible outcome will occur despite a lack of evidence. Part of the problem is that Beth has experienced overwhelming success in most areas of her life. She doesn't know how to handle the slightest disappointment and, as a result, her body reacts to any signs of possible failure. Let's see how Alan and Amy might help Beth overcome her fear and tolerate the idea of losing.

Understand and tolerate uncomfortable physical feelings. Just like automatic thoughts are our brains' way of telling us we're anxious, uncomfortable physical feelings are our bodies' way of doing the same thing. The first step is to help your child understand his physical feelings during social or performance anxiety–related situations. Young children like Isabelle may simply feel uncomfortable. They are less likely to understand that physical sensations can be connected to events they are anxious about. So, with a younger child, focus on breathing and relaxation exercises as coping strategies. Older children (and adolescents) like Beth are likely to experience a wider range of physical sensations, such as stomachaches, headaches, dizziness, and difficulty breathing. More important, they may also develop a *fear of fear*. This means that the child will become afraid to feel this way and will fear that a stomachache will invariably result in vomiting. The "Triple A's" can help your child be more in touch with, and more accepting of, his physical feelings (Eisen and Engler 2006):

- *Anticipate physical feelings during social or performance situations that provoke anxiety.* It's important to help your child learn to expect these physical feelings in situations that make him anxious, such as in a sports game, a music performance, or academic test. If he expects to feel sick while getting ready to perform, he may feel less scared when he actually experiences these feelings.

- *Accept physical feelings as a normal part of experiencing social or performance anxiety.* Help your child learn to tell himself that his physical feelings are the way his body communicates that he is nervous (for example, he could say, "It's just my anxiety"), and that he doesn't need to be afraid of them.

- *Appreciate the lack of connection between physical feelings and actual illness.* Help your child understand that his physical feelings are not a result of real physical illness. Over time, he will be able to recognize that feeling uncomfortable is related to anticipating an upcoming social or performance-based situation.

Develop a healthy attitude about playing competitive sports. Like any parent, you want your child to benefit from participating in competitive sports. You want him to work hard, develop skills, and, most important, have fun. Once your child masters the three A's, he will be less concerned about experiencing uncomfortable physical feelings, and he will be more able to enjoy sports with a healthy attitude. But what if he has gagged or vomited even once in the past? Like Beth, he will remain fearful, and this may interfere with his ability to develop a healthy attitude. In Stephen's case, it was enough to demonstrate that he didn't make mistakes very frequently. Beth, however, has a bigger hurdle preventing her from developing a healthy attitude toward sports—she needs to be able to cope in the face of what she sees as impending disaster.

Decatastrophize. You can help your child examine what would happen if his worst fear came true. Would it really be that bad? You can ask him the following evidence-based questions (Beck 1995; Kearney 2005):

- "What's the worst thing that could happen?"

- "If it has happened, was it really that bad?"

Alan and Amy helped Beth examine the evidence related to her experience of feeling physically ill during a competitive tennis match. They helped Beth realize that she had never actually vomited before, during, or after a match. Rather, she had become sick on two occasions, both of which were due to a stomach virus and had nothing to do with playing tennis. With their help, Beth did admit that becoming sick, although uncomfortable, had happened fast, and that she did actually feel better afterward. Your goal is to help your child realize that even the worst outcome is not really as bad as imagined and that it rarely occurs. Posing questions to your child this way (rather than reassuring him) helps to eliminate the fear of fear. Once your child stops focusing on the worst possible outcome, you can continue your inquiry with the following questions:

- "What usually happens [with regard to the child's feared event, such as getting sick]?"

- "What's the best thing that could happen?"

Alan and Amy helped Beth realize that she usually felt sick before a match, but that the feeling often subsided within the first thirty minutes of play. In addition, by regularly asking her "What's the best thing that could happen?" (with the answer being "Having no uncomfortable feelings"), Alan and Amy helped Beth start to focus on positive outcomes. It turned out that Beth was most nervous only when playing top players. By asking her a similar series of questions, Alan and Amy also helped lessen Beth's catastrophic fear of losing. For example, Beth soon realized that she rarely lost, and, even when she did, it wasn't without a major battle against players much older than her. Typically, however, she breezed through her matches without being challenged. Like Alan and Amy, you can help your child experience less anticipatory anxiety. But you're not done yet—you need to help your child to cope during stressful situations when things aren't going so well. For example, what would Beth do if she started to feel sick *during* a match and/or was on the verge of losing?

Develop coping thoughts.   It's one thing to help your child think in constructive ways before (minimizing anticipation) or after (making healthy self-evaluations) social or performance situations. But thinking rationally in the face of anxiety is no easy task. For this reason, you'll want to help prepare your child by teaching some coping thoughts to permit him to get through challenging situations more effectively. Coping thoughts are constructive ways of thinking about how to handle difficult situations. We illustrate below what Beth can say to herself when she feels sick or is losing a match.

Situation:	Feeling sick during competitive tennis match.
Automatic thoughts:	I feel sick ... What if I throw up?
Coping thoughts:	It's okay, it's just my anxiety ... Take a deep breath, practice the relaxation.

Situation:	On the verge of losing a competitive tennis match.
Automatic thoughts:	I'm losing ... I can't lose ...
Coping thoughts:	I'm doing the best I can ... I don't have to be perfect. I can't fail if I just keep trying.

The last step is to encourage healthy self-evaluations after your child's social or performance-based event, as Walter and Lorraine did with Stephen. Be sure to help your child emphasize his efforts, recognize his small successes, and develop an action plan for next time if overly disappointed. Help him focus on what he did well (rather than on his mistakes or any negative outcome) and the more enjoyable aspects of the competition. By doing so, over time, you will help lessen your child's self-imposed pressure to win and instead foster a healthier attitude about competition in general.

We'll now address the "social phobia" type as exemplified in the story of Paul and his parents, Stephanie and Arthur.

Paul: Making an Effort

As you may remember, Paul is a soft-spoken, sensitive, and intelligent thirteen-year-old boy. He does well in school and has some friends. Paul has always been socially anxious and cautious around others. But lately he has been having trouble attending school on exam days and is increasingly reluctant to socialize with both friends and family, due to his worries about being the center of attention. He fears he will be scrutinized or will do something that will cause himself embarrassment or humiliation. Stephanie and Arthur are puzzled that Paul is acting this way. After all, he has never reported any unpleasant social experiences. They just want him to be able to live his life without so much worry and anxiety.

Stephanie and Arthur want Paul to be able to do the following:

- Attend school on days when he must perform (tests, oral presentations)

- Make an effort to more regularly socialize with friends and family

Let's take a look at Paul's list of goals, which could serve as possible exposures.

Paul's List for Discovering the Truth

School Situations

- Spend time in cafeteria

- Attend classes on test dates

- Work in groups

- Give an oral presentation

Social Situations

- Use public bathrooms

- Attend movies

- Eat in restaurants

- Visit malls

Like Beth, Paul is worried about experiencing disastrous outcomes. For this reason, Paul can benefit from many of the cognitive and relaxation-based strategies discussed earlier in this chapter. But Paul is not simply concerned about losing the approval of others, performing poorly, or becoming physically ill. Rather, he worries that others are talking about him. He doesn't want to be the center of attention. His worst fear is that at any given moment he may do something, such as panic, and "all eyes" would then be focused on him. Paul's list of feared situations contains school and social settings, and in putting himself in these situations he will find out that there is very little, if any, chance that he will do something embarrassing. But helping him to learn this is no easy task. Paul is completely convinced that humiliation is inevitable. This brings us to our next guiding principle, *be persistent*.

Be Persistent

Stephanie and Arthur have always left Paul's social life up to him. Now they realize that he needs some help but are not sure how to intervene. Paul strongly resists any encouragement on their part, and we can see why he does so—unlike Beth's social anxiety, which is restricted to competitive tennis, Paul's social phobia is stronger and generalized across many social situations. Thinking about and participating in all of these potentially embarrassing situations is utterly exhausting. Paul's only chance for relief is to avoid all social situations completely.

But what Paul doesn't realize is that he simply needs to go to a mall or restaurant, work in a group, or spend time in the school cafeteria, even for brief intervals, to find out that he won't be embarrassed. Stephanie and Arthur will need to be persistent in their support of Paul's small steps toward attending social situations. They need to be firm in their stand, making it clear to Paul that completely avoiding school or social situations is not an option.

Like Isabelle and Beth, Paul also struggles with key cognitive distortions, but his most notable distortions include fortune telling and mind reading. Paul automatically assumes that attending any social situation will result in his embarrassment and/or humiliation, even though he lacks evidence from his past social experiences (fortune telling). He keeps thinking that the next time will be truly embarrassing. His inaccurate fortune telling is directly related to his inaccurate mind reading. For instance, even though the teacher praised his oral presentation, Paul felt embarrassed since he believed that others had noticed his trembling hands and shaky voice. Paul has to learn that not everyone is thinking about, judging, or interested in his actions. Let's see how Stephanie and Arthur can accomplish their goals for Paul.

Attend school on performance-based days (tests, oral presentations). If your child or adolescent is like Paul, it's especially important that he attend school, especially for mandatory events like tests. Remember, thinking about being embarrassed is always worse than any actual outcome—if your child stays home from school, he believes that he has surely avoided a social disaster. You need to make sure he gets to school on those days when he needs to take a test, so he can find out that there is no such disaster. Of course, you'll need to expect some resistance on your child's part.

> *Preserve your child's sense of control.* The idea is to challenge your child, but at the same time not overwhelm him (Eisen and Engler 2006). If he feels too insecure, he may refuse to go to school at all on performance or test days. To help him feel in control, try working out an arrangement with his teacher(s) ahead of time, which might allow him to do any of the following:
>
> - Attend school (but be excused from a specific class)
>
> - Attend class (observing rather than participating)
>
> - Take the test in an isolated room

The first step is to help your child willingly go to school. If your child is like Paul, he is not worried about performing poorly; he is more concerned that others will notice his nervousness or that he will do something embarrassing. And his worry will only grow as long as he's allowed to stay home from school. Once at school, he will gradually feel more secure and will ultimately participate. Allow your child to progress at his own pace, completing exposures, one at a time, that will eventually lead to his attending school with full participation. However, because of his cognitive distortions, we still need to help him more accurately interpret these exposures. After all, his way of thinking is inhibiting his socialization. Read on for ways to help him sort out his distortions and free him up to participate in social situations.

Make an effort to more regularly socialize with friends and family. Sometimes, having a social phobia can actually make a child or adolescent feel important. How would you feel if you thought everyone was interested in your thoughts, feelings, and actions, even in a negative way? If all of that interest is giving him a false sense of importance, which is perpetuating his phobia, then you'll need to help your child realize that most people are not thinking about him—and, in fact, that they don't have the time to care.

Help your child become less self-focused (Kearney 2005) about his anxiety and diminish his worry about being judged by using the following sequence of real-life exposures.

1. Walk through an unfamiliar mall or other crowded place where no one will recognize him. Keep track of individuals who look at, stare at, or attempt to talk to either one of you. Help your child realize that everyone is going about their own business. Repeat this process at increasingly familiar settings.

2. Attend an unfamiliar restaurant simply to observe others. If your child is like Paul (who worries that he will be recognized, that he will make a mistake like spilling his drink, or that others will make comments about what and how he eats), he will be agreeable as long as he doesn't have to eat. Watch what happens if someone makes a mistake. What does your child think about that person? Help him realize that he, like everyone else, is not overly concerned with the actions of others and is forgiving as well. Repeat this process at increasingly familiar restaurants, until he can eat something comfortably with minimal fear.

3. Videotape your child during a social event (party or family gathering) or performance-related event (such as a sports game, concert, or spelling bee). Be sure to get footage of your child alone, your child interacting

with others, and isolated spectators. Discuss his reaction to watching himself (he may see himself as visibly nervous), how you think he comes across (you will probably see him as looking fairly calm), and other people's responses (they will likely seem neutral or uninterested). Help him realize that, despite his beliefs, his anxiety is hardly, if at all, noticeable. If he remains unconvinced, have him watch the footage with other supportive family members or friends, and get their feedback as well.

4. Implement naturally occurring social situations or events. Be firm regarding your child or adolescent's attendance or participation when he gets invited to social events. Make it clear that, unless your family has previous plans, he must at the very least attend the event. (Leaving it up to him may still result in excuses not to be there.) Over time, help him work toward making these decisions on his own. Do not present this step until he has successfully completed the previous exposures.

5. Encourage your child or adolescent to take initiative to be more social, first with family members, and then with his friends. Take small steps (starting with phone calls or e-mail messages) and allow him to progress at his own pace as long as he continues to make an effort on a regular basis.

Remember, overcoming social phobia is a process that takes time. By following our guidelines, you can help your child or adolescent gradually eliminate his social avoidance, cope more effectively in social or performance situations, and most important, develop healthy thinking and relationships.

Summary

In this chapter, we've guided you through our step-by-step plans for helping your child manage the key forms of shyness or social anxiety. More important, we've set the stage for fostering his assertiveness, confidence, and ability to cope with stressful social situations. In chapter 6, we'll show you how to help your child overcome his social withdrawal with our real-life stories of Jessica, George, and their parents.

Recommended Resources

Carducci, B. 2003. *The Shyness Breakthrough*. New York: Rodale.

Friedberg, R., and J. McClure. 2002. *Clinical Practice of Cognitive Therapy with Children and Adolescents*. New York: Guilford Press.

Last, C. 2005. *Help for Worried Kids*. New York: Guilford Press.

Rapee, R., S. Spence, V. Cobham, and A. Wignall. 2000. *Helping Your Anxious Child*. Oakland, CA: New Harbinger Publications.

6

What to Do When Your Child Is Socially Withdrawn

For the first time, George is showing some interest in activities and learning to help himself.

—Beverly

Chapter Objectives

In this chapter you will learn the following:

- Guiding principles to help your child become more socially active

- How to plan a step-by-step program based on your child's unique social needs

- Specific coping strategies for managing the key forms of social withdrawal in children and adolescents

Helping Your Child Cope with Social Withdrawal

Children with social anxiety often want to be with their peers, but because of shyness, self-consciousness, performance anxiety, and/or a fear of humiliation they frequently avoid unfamiliar social situations. For instance, as you recall, Paul has a desire to be with people, but he worries about socializing with friends and family because of the possibility of doing something that will cause him embarrassment or humiliation. Paul's avoidance is anxiety related: he wishes to escape discomfort.

Social withdrawal, however, is more about choosing to isolate oneself from both familiar and unfamiliar people and situations, about wanting to be alone. Social withdrawal, in its mildest form, may result from a preference for solitary activities, as we see with Jessica. But more typically, however, it stems from a combination of social anxiety and depressive features, which George demonstrates.

We begin by illustrating our step-by-step plan to help Jessica become more socially active.

Jessica: Becoming Reengaged

As you may recall from chapter 2, Jessica is a sensitive twelve-year-old girl. She does well in school and is liked by her peers. Other than going to school, however, she rarely leaves her room at home. Lately, she has been making excuses not to attend social events such as birthday parties and family get-togethers. Ann is worried that Jessica's social development is falling behind that of her peers, and that if she doesn't reengage soon she will start losing her friends. But any encouragement on Ann's part leads to one big power struggle.

If your child is like Jessica, you likely have several goals in mind for her, such as the following:

- Take initiative (and reciprocate) with other children

- Participate in organized activities

- Be more agreeable when asked to participate

Let's take a look at Jessica's list of social activities to work toward, which could serve as possible exposures.

Jessica's Social Activities List

Neighborhood Activities

- Visit a friend (planned or spontaneous)

- Invite a friend to come over

Social Events

- Attend obligatory family and peer events

- Initiate and reciprocate peer contacts (via phone calls, e-mails)

- Invite peers to socialize (at least two times per week)

Extracurricular Activities

- Observe, then attend peer-related recreational activities

- Participate in one organized activity (such as sports, music, or a club)

Like Isabelle (see chapter 5), Jessica is also slow to warm up temperamentally and, as such, is apprehensive about taking initiative with her peers and participating in structured group activities. For this reason, Jessica can benefit from a program similar to Isabelle's. But Jessica's social anxiety is only a bit of an obstacle, because she simply prefers solitary activities.

At the same time, Jessica doesn't like confrontations of any kind and views them as intrusions to her privacy. As a result, Jessica has learned that it's easier to be agreeable than express her opinions with her friends. Although such a tactic is not always ideal, it has helped Jessica become immediately likeable. At home, however, she feels safe, and, being strong willed, does not respond well to Ann's demands that she be more social. This brings us to our next guiding principle, *be mindful of your demands on your child.*

Be Mindful of Your Demands

Ann is frustrated by Jessica's confusing social behavior. Jessica appears to enjoy talking to her friends on the phone when they call her. The other kids flock to her at school and she gets invited to a lot of parties. So why does Jessica refuse to pick up the phone to call anyone, and why does she make excuses for not participating in any organized activities?

On one hand, Ann and Ron are grateful that Jessica works hard in school and is an excellent student, and so both parents are careful not to overwhelm her with other responsibilities. However, Ann and Ron differ in their views of Jessica's peer relationships. Ann cannot help but feel concerned that Jessica is falling behind her peers socially because she is spending so much time alone. Ron, on the other hand, has always been on the timid side and fully expects Jessica to "come out of her shell" in due time as he did. Jessica just wants to be left alone. She feels that she has enough friends, and she socializes when she feels like it. She doesn't understand why her mother has to be so intrusive. Ann and Jessica both have valid points.

First, Ann is correct that it's unhealthy for Jessica to completely withdraw. If she continues to do so, Jessica could lose her friends. But just like Walter cannot force Stephen to develop a "killer instinct" (see chapter 5), Ann cannot force Jessica to become more socially active. Second, Jessica is right that her mom puts too much pressure on her to socialize, but it's not okay for Jessica to simply do nothing. Her social life is just as important as her schoolwork. Third, the fact that Ron understands what it's like to be timid doesn't mean that he should just sit back and hope that Jessica becomes more social. After all, given his experience, he is in an excellent position to help facilitate her social well-being. Balance and compromise on everyone's part is needed. Let's see how Ann and Ron go about helping Jessica participate more often in social activities.

Take initiative (and reciprocate) with other children. As is the case with Paul, it's very important to preserve Jessica's sense of control. If she perceives too much pressure to socialize, she will become resentful and withdraw further.

> *Set some reasonable limits.* You want to provide a structure that allows your child to develop social initiative but is flexible enough to foster her sense of independence. Have your child gradually assume more responsibility for the following assignments, adding one assignment each week. Be sure to discuss your goals and realistic expectations up front.
>
> 1. Initiate two social contacts per week (phone, e-mail, or in-person conversation), one of which must be a phone call. These contacts are purely for touching base and can be about any topic; such a conversation could even start as a request for clarification on a homework assignment, for example, and then perhaps evolve into a chat about another social topic, like a movie both kids have seen. Remember, leaving messages on answering machines counts. Emphasize taking initiative rather than the amount of time actually spent interacting with others.
>
> 2. Return peer phone calls or e-mail within forty-eight hours. Although twenty-four hours would be ideal, it's better to start out by being flexible. In the beginning of the program, one or two prompts on your part may be necessary.
>
> 3. Extend two invitations to socialize per week (via phone, e-mail, or in-person conversation). Remember, it's not crucial that these invitations result in actual playdates or visits. Rather, it's more important that your child make the effort. Over time, peer contacts will naturally become more frequent. Of course, it's ideal for her to extend invitations to two different peers, but, in the beginning, as long as she makes

an effort, attempting to connect with one peer is fine. Don't be surprised if she leaves her assignments until the end of the week—because of discomfort, she may procrastinate. Unfortunately, by doing so, she may sabotage her chances of getting together with her peers. Rather than letting your frustrations get the best of you, simply set a midweek deadline for making the necessary arrangements.

4. Chart progress. Create a chart that allows your child to very easily document her daily or weekly social initiatives. Remember, if your child is strong willed like Jessica, any encouragement on your part may be perceived as unpleasant nagging and cause her to withdraw further. Allowing your child to chart her own progress eliminates potential power struggles and encourages social independence. Place the chart in a neutral area like your kitchen so you can unobtrusively check her monitoring. Schedule an agreed-upon time at the end of the week to discuss her progress, but avoid discussing it too often, since this may undermine her efforts. Be forgiving and emphasize partial successes—focus on what she is doing (which is more than she did before) rather than what she is not doing (such as forgetting to monitor or lapsing in her efforts). Shape her behavior and use contingent rewards as needed.

You have now created a structure to help your child become more socially active. As she progresses toward these goals, you can take a step back, and she will likely perceive your actions as less intrusive than before. Once she becomes accustomed to taking social initiative regularly, you will be in a better position to help her accomplish the next goal.

Participate in organized activities. In your efforts to help your child socialize more frequently, you've created the understanding (without the power struggles) between the two of you that this is something she needs to do. Let's continue to help your child progress by setting another reasonable limit.

Pick an activity, any activity. If Ann had her way, Jessica would be participating in a variety of organized weekly activities. Ron, however, feels it should be left up to Jessica. Ann's and Ron's opposing points of view are giving Jessica mixed messages. And it's not surprising that Jessica takes the easier way out. Before they do anything, Ann and Ron need to agree to work together to encourage, support, and sustain Jessica's participation in an organized activity until completion.

Once you and your spouse or partner come to such an agreement, conduct a family brainstorming session with your child. Devise a list of healthy organized activities, preferably group-oriented ones that your child has expressed interest in at one time or another. If she is overly resistant to this idea, consider more individual extracurricular activities (such as one-on-one music or sports lessons). To preserve her sense of control, let your child make the choice. Be firm that doing nothing is not an option, but at the same time be flexible regarding her initial level of participation. Of course, no matter how you proceed, she will resist. How much so depends on her temperament (strong willed versus passive) and the amount of time since she last participated in an organized activity. Rather than responding to her emotional reaction, try to shape her behavior and set a reasonable deadline for her to make a decision.

Change the dynamic (Eisen and Schaefer 2005). If Ann were the parent enforcing Jessica's participation in organized activities, Jessica would forcefully resist or simply withdraw further. Instead, they will change the dynamic, so now Ron will take the lead in helping Jessica participate. This change is less likely to result in a power struggle. The fact that the directive comes from Ron, given his own history of timidity and lack of limit setting, tells Jessica that her participation has tremendous value. In any event, it's important that spouses or partners be united when helping their children become more socially active.

Become more agreeable when asked to participate. Another strategy to help defuse possible power struggles with your child and to foster greater cooperation is to validate her concerns. As a parent, you have the right to set limits. But every child yearns to feel validated in the face of those limits. Your child doesn't have to like or graciously accept your demands. But she is more likely to cooperate if she feels heard and understood. Expecting her to obey your wishes without some kind of justification or explanation (for instance, simply saying "Because I said so") doesn't work well. Let's take a look at how Ann and Ron validate Jessica's reluctance to participate in their local soccer league, once she has selected soccer as the activity she will try:

Ann: We know that you're not enthusiastic about playing soccer, but you've played before, many of your friends have signed up, and you chose this activity. We feel it would be good for you to participate.

Jessica: I didn't choose anything! You made me choose from that list of activities. There are too many people at the soccer games. Why can't you just leave me alone?!

Ron: We understand that it's not your favorite thing to do. If you feel uncomfortable during a soccer game or practice, take a few deep breaths. Remember, we made a deal. We would very much like you to try. You're a good soccer player.

Jessica: [*long pause, deep sigh*] Oh, all right. But this is the last time.

Children like Jessica have mild social anxiety, but they also possess adequate social skills and can participate in organized activities successfully. Despite your child's lack of interest in doing so, you can help her become more socially balanced with minimal power struggles if you take a united, supportive, and firm stance. It's a different story, however, if your adolescent is like George and experiences strong social anxiety and social withdrawal.

George: Becoming Enthusiastic

As you may remember from chapter 2, George is a mildly overweight and sensitive fifteen-year-old boy who rarely talks to his peers or teachers at school. On days when tests or group presentations are given, George refuses to attend school. George complains of being bored all the time, having low energy, and experiencing frequent headaches and concentration difficulties. And lately, he has become even more pessimistic about school and peers ("What's the point?"). Despite having a handful of friends, he expresses minimal interest in being social and no longer cares about his schoolwork. George also has lost interest in family-oriented activities.

Beverly and Herbert want George to be able to do the following:

- Become more energetic

- Show some interest in family, peer, and school activities

- Develop some social contacts

Let's take a look at the goals George's parents set for him, which could serve as a list of possible exposures.

George's Social Connections List

School and Social Situations

- Talk to peers and teachers

- Attend gym class

- Use the bathroom at school

- Attend classes on test dates

- Give an oral or group presentation

Social Events

- Attend obligatory family and peer events

- Initiate and reciprocate peer contacts

Since George experiences many of the same social concerns as do Beth (performance anxiety), Paul (social phobia), and Jessica (lack of social initiative), he can benefit from many of the strategies designed to help them. But unlike these other children, George's social withdrawal is more pronounced. His pessimistic attitude, unhealthy diet, and limited interest in doing anything are communicating important messages to his parents. In order to get George back on track, before making any efforts to get him more socially connected, his parents will want to note an important guiding principle: *be mindful of your child's signals.*

Be Mindful of Your Child's Signals

Beverly and Herbert need to become more involved in George's life—and that is what his behaviors seem to be communicating. Their lack of involvement is no fault of their own and may be due to a number of reasons. Both parents must work full-time, and as a result, they have expected George to assume greater responsibility for his schoolwork and social well-being. In addition, George's tendency toward social withdrawal means that he does not usually demand or encourage regular family contact and emotional intimacy. Most important, recognizing the signs of social withdrawal and/or depression is not easy; these are often expressed through a lack of energy, appetite and sleep problems, and somatic complaints, rather than through sadness, crying, or other, more expected symptoms. These physical features are often overlooked and not recognized as characteristics of social withdrawal and/or depression.

Also making it difficult to identify George's depression and social withdrawal is the fact that cognitive symptoms such as negative thoughts, guilt, or feelings of inadequacy are more likely to emerge during adolescence. However, because of shifting social allegiances (from parents to peers) and greater needs for privacy and independence at this age, parents are often left in the dark. Like many parents, Beverly and Herbert have been seeing George's increasingly pessimistic attitude and withdrawal from family activities as a sign of impending adolescence.

Adolescents' grades, eating habits, and sleeping patterns are also sometimes difficult for parents to sort out, since it's not always clear what's normal and what isn't. Most parents aren't even aware of their children's slipping grades until the end of a marking period. Given George's history of academic excellence, Beverly and Herbert have had no reason to expect anything less than high grades from him. They have also not been fully aware of George's dietary issues (skipping meals, and snacking late at night), simply attributing his eating habits to "pickiness." They have become concerned, however, that he is overweight and have considered contacting a nutritionist. Similarly, they are concerned that George is "tired all the time," but they largely attribute his lack of energy to his frequent afternoon napping, thinking that he should develop a more regular sleep cycle.

Beverly and Herbert need to become more mindful of George's signals—for instance, how he communicates his sadness and social withdrawal. But before they can do that, they'll need to take him for a physical examination in order to be sure that his lack of energy, appetite problems, and sleep disturbances are not due to physical illness.

Before we move on to how Beverly and Herbert can accomplish their goals for helping George, there's one other issue we should consider. Let's take a moment to think about some signs of depression that George does *not* seem to be exhibiting: he has not made any statements about hopelessness, guilt, or death. If your socially withdrawn or depressed child or adolescent is expressing any of these kinds of thoughts, or if you feel concerned and can't really explain why, please turn immediately to chapter 9 to learn whether you should be contacting a professional, before attempting to address your child's symptoms on your own.

Now, let's see how Beverly and Herbert help George get more energy, feel better, and initiate some social connections.

Become more energetic. An important first step is to find more energy. A lack of energy ultimately affects the child's mood, motivation, and ability to make and sustain social connections. Before we assume that this lethargy is emotional, we need to examine the impact of any contributing physical factors, such as irregular sleep, lack of exercise, and/or unhealthy eating habits.

> *Develop good sleep habits.* Think of the last time that you had difficulty sleeping over the course of a few days or weeks. What were you like at home and/or work? You were probably irritable, felt impatient, and had trouble focusing. We need our sleep if we are to function at optimal levels. The average adolescent requires nine hours of sleep. Daytime sleepiness results from inconsistent or inadequate sleep and is associated with less positive mood, irritability, temper outbursts, and greater attention and concentration difficulties. A vicious cycle of fatigue, moodiness, sleepiness, and anxiety can easily develop. George's sleep cycle has been disrupted due to long naps during the day and frequent night waking.
>
> The first order of business for George was to help him develop a regular sleep-wake cycle. Beverly and Herbert set some reasonable limits for George's bedtime. If your adolescent is strong willed and resists an enforced bedtime, focus more on the morning routine. For instance, to help maintain George's sense of control, Beverly and Herbert decided to be flexible regarding his bedtime, as long as George awakened easily in the morning and got ready for school on time. More important, they eliminated the afternoon naps by gradually reducing their frequency and duration, so George would stay up all afternoon and go to bed earlier at night. Once your child's naps are eliminated, chart her progress noting the approximate time she falls asleep each night, the frequency and duration of any night wakings, and the number of times (weekly) she sleeps through the night. Her anxiety and/or mood may be getting the best of her if appreciable progress is not evident within two weeks. If this is the case, you may need to develop a more structured nighttime routine that benefits the whole family.

Beverly and Herbert could see that they needed to spend time with George, but, more important, they needed to listen to his feelings of sadness and anxiety. For this reason, after dinner each night (following completion of homework), they created an open family forum, where each person was given an opportunity to vent frustrations, worries, negative thoughts, and sad feelings without being judged or criticized. Family members simply listened to, acknowledged, or validated each other's concerns. As you can imagine, this was not easy for George, so Beverly and Herbert took the lead and shared their own personal concerns until George was ready to participate. If you establish such a forum, once your adolescent vents her emotions the rest of the evening can be devoted to activities that are relaxing (taking a bath or shower, and practicing breathing or relaxation exercises) and pleasantly distracting (listening to music or reading). Avoid overly stimulating activities such as video games or television.

Like irregular sleep, infrequent exercise is also associated with fatigue. Approximately 15 percent of children and adolescents are overweight and lack of exercise is an important contributing factor. Youth who do not exercise presumably spend too much time at the computer, playing video games, or watching television. Regular exercise is associated with better mood, attitude, sleep, and ability to cope with stress. In fact, research suggests that active adolescents feel less lonely, shy, and hopeless.

Exercise regularly. Being overweight themselves, Beverly and Herbert knew that an exercise regimen needed to be a family affair. For this reason, the family joined a local gym. At first, George refused to go, out of fear of being recognized by his peers and due to embarrassment about his weight. He did agree, however, to taking brisk walks with Beverly three mornings per week. If necessary, you might consider contingent rewards to get your adolescent started. Once George was feeling a bit better about his body, he agreed to attend personal training sessions at off hours, which ultimately led to regular gym visits on his own. George also signed up for private tennis and swimming lessons. Work toward having your adolescent join a low-pressure group-oriented recreational activity such as soccer, basketball, hiking, or biking. Make regular exercise an important part of your family's lifestyle. Doing so will reduce stress, enhance your adolescent's body image and self-esteem, and improve overall family well-being.

In addition to adequate sleep and regular exercise, a balanced diet is an important part of your adolescent's wellness plan. Because of our hectic lifestyles, we sometimes miss meals or eat unhealthy foods. Doing so on a regular basis can easily upset our mood, energy level, and ability to concentrate, and it can result in weight gain. By regularly skipping breakfast and lunch and eating sugary snacks late at night, George was unknowingly wreaking havoc on his blood sugar levels, leaving him feeling tired, weak, and irritable during the day and overly alert at night. George's diet was in great need of regulation.

Eat healthy foods.   Helping George develop a healthy diet was another way that Beverly and Herbert could listen to their son's signals. George skipped meals or picked at his food during the day because of physical discomfort (social anxiety about school) or a lack of appetite (sad mood). So, along with their family forum, they made family breakfasts and dinners a priority. These meals became comfortable, predictable times to share news, ideas, and events as well as to ensure healthy eating habits for all family members. In addition, while cleaning up after dinner, Beverly helped George prepare satisfying but healthy lunches.

The hardest part, of course, was the task of eliminating George's nighttime snacking. Since Beverly and Herbert were often asleep in the middle of the night and were unable to supervise George's nighttime eating, Beverly decided to limit the availability of unhealthy snacks in their home, replacing them with healthier alternatives, such as fruits and whole grain foods. As you can imagine, George was most upset about this idea, but so was Herbert, who also enjoyed his snacks. Beverly and Herbert consulted a nutritionist, who ultimately planned George's daily menus in a flexible fashion. Getting the help of a nutritionist is an excellent idea if your child or adolescent is overweight, and, as an added benefit, defuses those unpleasant food-related power struggles between parent and child. This is especially true for children or adolescents who may be susceptible to developing eating disorders such as anorexia and bulimia. (If you are concerned that your child may be on the path to developing an eating disorder, it is important to contact your child's physician or an eating disorders specialist in your area.)

Once your adolescent has more energy, you can then help her accomplish the next goal.

Show some interest in family, peer, and school activities.   At this point, your adolescent may now have some energy to actually think about becoming involved in family, peer, and school activities. The problem, however, may be her pessimistic, gloomy outlook ("What's the point?" she may say). Socially withdrawn and depressed youth tend to think negatively about themselves, others, and the environment (Kendall and MacDonald 1993). Unlike anxious youth, who have both positive and negative thoughts, depressed youth often lack the positive ones; this is another cognitive distortion, in which the positive gets discounted, and the negative remains and is viewed as a reflection of personal inadequacies. Thinking this way encourages depression and low self-esteem.

> *Reattribution.* Help your adolescent learn to become more optimistic by making attributions of failure less personal and evaluating situations in more positive, neutral, or accurate ways. Beverly used the following reattribution technique (Seligman et al. 1995) when George refused to attend school on exam days.

Overly personal and inaccurate interpretation → threatens self-esteem

---

George: I can't go to school today. Last time, I was so
          nervous I didn't finish the test. Why bother?
          I'm such a loser.

Reattribute to a less personal and external cause

Beverly: Why didn't you finish the test?

George: I was up all night.

Beverly: Does that make you a loser?

George: [*sighs*] No, just tired.

Overly general and inaccurate interpretation
     → encourages failure across situations

George: But Mom, you know I can't focus whenever other
          people are around. It's too much for me.

Reattribute to a more specific set of circumstances

Beverly: I know you get nervous, but do you really have
          trouble focusing during tests?

George: [*looks surprised*] I think so ...

Beverly: What was your lowest grade this marking period?

George: [*speaks softly*] 92.

Beverly: Can you focus during tests when other people are
          around?

George: I guess so. [*half smiles*]

Beverly: Is it really too much for you?

George: I guess not, but I definitely can't handle speaking in front of others.

Overly rigid and inaccurate interpretation
→ leaves no room for improvement

George: I'm never giving another oral presentation. I'm not going through that again.

Reattribute to more optimistic future outcomes

Beverly: How many times have you dropped your note cards?

George: Once.

Beverly: Did you recover?

George: Yes ...

Beverly: Were the other students forgiving?

George: [*sighs, nods head*]

Beverly: What can you say to yourself?

George: I'll do better the next time.

Schedule pleasant events.   Once your adolescent has a bit of energy, is thinking in a more optimistic way, and starts participating in family-oriented activities, you can help schedule pleasant events for her (Barnard 2003). We all need access to pleasant and reinforcing situations. This is our best defense against passivity, social withdrawal, and depression. Pleasant events not only enhance our mood, but they also keep negativity at bay, by virtue of distraction.

George had begun walking with his mom, going to the gym, and participating in occasional family outings. Even though he was feeling better, he still viewed these events as obligatory, rarely expressed interest in them, and showed minimal initiative. For this reason, Beverly and Herbert kept things simple and scheduled at least one pleasant event per week that George had previously found enjoyable. Considering his social phobia, his initial list was short and included visiting the library, town bookstore, and hobby shop during off hours.

In scheduling pleasant events for your child or adolescent, be sure not to overwhelm her. Your goal is to help stir her interest in desirable events, but, more important, to steer her away from isolating and sedentary activities, such as watching television or playing video games, that encourage further withdrawal. Always take into account her degree of social anxiety and/or social withdrawal when deciding the frequency and intensity of the activities. Before, during, and after these events, help her to affirm the positive aspects of the situation—for instance, finding something pleasant to say, no matter how insignificant. Regular positive self-statements (such as "I had a good time" or even "The weather was nice") will counteract and eventually minimize her negative remarks (such as "Nothing is fun" and "What a waste of time") that contribute to depression and social withdrawal.

Beverly and Herbert also took advantage of competence-enhancing activities to help preserve George's sense of self-worth. They took turns playing games with George, choosing ones that he excelled at, such as chess and backgammon. Doing so not only created more family time but also helped George feel a sense of mastery and well-being.

Develop some social contacts. Once your adolescent accomplishes the first two goals, you can help her take social initiative, as Ann and Ron did with Jessica. But if your adolescent experiences strong social anxiety, withdrawal, and/or depressive features, like George did, it's best to help her develop social contacts as a first step rather than immediately pursuing social invitations. Be firm, but be sure to preserve her sense of control as you implement the program described earlier in this chapter for Jessica.

It's important to remember that your child has likely been socially withdrawn for some time, and she may need to venture out into the social world in very small steps. Thus, with your love and support, she can gradually redevelop an interest in others, become increasingly socially active, and learn to think in more optimistic ways.

Summary

In this chapter, we've guided you through our step-by-step plans for managing the key forms of social withdrawal. In chapters 7 and 8, we'll return to the children in our real-life stories, who, in addition to exhibiting social anxiety and/or social withdrawal, also experience underlying neurological issues that make them more prone to neglect and rejection by their peers. In chapter 7 we'll focus on the children who are more likely to be neglected, and then in chapter 8 we'll address the children who are more likely to be rejected and even bullied. Let's move on to chapter 7, where we'll show you how to help your child become less vulnerable and more socially competent with our real-life stories of Ralph and Tracey and their parents.

Recommended Resources

Barnard, M. 2003. *Helping Your Depressed Child*. Oakland, CA: New Harbinger Publications.

Eisen, A., and L. Engler. 2006. *Helping Your Child Overcome Separation Anxiety or School Refusal*. Oakland, CA: New Harbinger Publications.

Kearney, C. 2001. *School Refusal Behavior in Youth*. Washington, DC: American Psychological Association.

7

What to Do When
Your Child Is Socially
Vulnerable and Neglected

Ralph and I went to the driving range and he actually asked for my help with his swing! We had such a pleasant time together.

—Len

Chapter Objectives

In this chapter you will learn the following:

- Guiding principles to help your child become more socially competent

- How to implement a step-by-step program based on your child's unique social needs

- Specific coping strategies for managing the key forms of social vulnerability likely to lead to peer neglect

Many socially vulnerable children struggle with social anxiety and/or social withdrawal but also suffer from neurological problems in addition to their social difficulties. This blend of symptoms often results in undesirable behavioral and/or personality characteristics that alienate other children and further increase the child's vulnerability.

Our focus in this chapter is to help you identify your child's unique social needs (for instance, to become more tolerant or responsible) and help him compensate for these deficits with an individualized program of skills-based strategies. In this chapter, we'll guide you through the key forms of social vulnerability that can lead to peer neglect, using Ralph and Tracey as examples. In chapter 8 we will focus on socially vulnerable youngsters who are more actively rejected by their peers. Let's begin with Ralph and his parents, Elaine and Len.

Ralph: Learning Tolerance

As you may recall from chapters 2 and 3, Ralph is a sensitive, serious, and irritable eleven-year-old boy who doesn't see his contribution to negative situations, doesn't see anything as his fault ("I didn't do anything wrong"), and believes everyone else is mean. His parents find themselves engaged in frequent power struggles with him—over even the smallest tasks—which often end with him claiming that his parents hate him. Elaine and Len just wish Ralph would lighten up a bit and try participating in social activities again. Using their answers to Ralph's social vulnerability checklist (see chapter 3), Elaine and Len have chosen the following goals for Ralph:

Ralph's Taking-Ownership Goals

- Develop a better attitude

- Accept responsibility for his actions

As is the case with our other real-life stories, our overarching goal is to help Ralph become more socially active and successful. But

Ralph is dealing with some underlying neurological issues (pragmatic learning challenges), in addition to his social anxiety and social withdrawal, that make attaining this goal more difficult for him—and will make him more vulnerable to being neglected by his peers. In order to improve his social success, Ralph ultimately needs to learn how to become more aware of how his behavior affects others. Naturally, Elaine and Len will need to take into account his pragmatic learning struggles as they go about helping him, following an important guiding principle: *be mindful of your child's burden.*

Be Mindful of Your Child's Burden

It's not surprising that Elaine and Len are frustrated with Ralph's overly negative attitude and behavior. Elaine remarks, "Ralph manages to find something negative about everything that he does. He complains that he has too much homework, that the kids at school are mean, and that we hate him. I wish he would stop saying that; it's just not true. I don't understand. We bend over backward to please him, but everything is a power struggle. Ralph doesn't seem to appreciate anything that we do for him, but he never forgets the times when we're too busy to help him. Maybe I try too hard to make him happy, but I think sitting around all day and watching television is not healthy. He never wants to do anything. He's either too tired or some part of his body is hurting."

Len agrees. "I'm trying to help Ralph become a better golfer but he won't accept my feedback, and lately he'd rather just stay home. Any time I suggest doing something, he tells me that he hates to do that. It irks me that he always says 'I didn't do anything wrong' even when it's obvious that he did. He never thinks it's his fault. He just doesn't get it, and the other kids are starting to notice. He always looks like he took a bite out of a sour apple. He's a sweet kid and deserves to have friends. I wish he could become a little more tolerant."

Elaine and Len are right—Ralph is not easy to be around. But that's not his fault. He's not intentionally being overly rigid and difficult. Because of his pragmatic learning challenges, he has trouble understanding and interpreting the meaning of certain types of spoken language (such as sarcasm) and reading nonverbal (social) cues. It's as if he's wandering aimlessly in a foreign country. He has neither a road map nor a knowledge of the language. In other words, he's completely lost. Trying to make sense of his world is frustrating and exhausting. This is one reason why he is overly negative and tired. Another reason is that he struggles with two cognitive distortions, negative filter and overestimating.

Ralph's negative filter causes him to have a tendency to focus on the negative features of situations or events. His habitual overestimation prevents him from even attempting some activities, because in his mind there is a much greater chance of unpleasant outcomes than there actually is. If your child is like Ralph, it's important that you accept and understand his burden, which is the result of his pragmatic learning challenges. By doing so, you will minimize feelings of resentment on your part, and his behavior will seem less personal and intentional. Let's look at how Elaine and Len accomplish their goals for Ralph.

Develop a better attitude. The first step in helping Ralph develop a better attitude is to teach him how to more accurately interpret other people's body language, such as facial expressions or gestures.

Understanding other people's body language. Our faces and gestures convey a tremendous amount of information regarding our thoughts, feelings, and emotions. But facial expressions can be subtle and easily misinterpreted, which can lead to misunderstandings or worse in many different situations, such as poker. Picking up nonverbal signals is an important skill in poker, and the best poker players are experts at reading others' body language. For instance, facial movements such as licking lips, flaring nostrils, stroking the face, or tapping the table repeatedly with any regularity give hints to the kind of hand a person is holding. Guessing wrong too often can be costly. The same is true for children when they regularly misinterpret their peers' or family members' body language. For example, when Ralph looks at Elaine's face and sees that she has a neutral expression (looking neither happy nor sad), he frequently thinks that she is mad at him. She repeatedly tells Ralph, "That's just my face," but Ralph automatically assumes she's upset. The same is true with his peers. Ralph quickly withdraws when they don't immediately respond to his greetings with friendly facial expressions. His self-absorption causes him to expect others to just stop what they're doing and focus on him, as in the following example, in which Elaine is talking on the phone in the kitchen when Ralph walks in, wanting her attention:

Ralph: Mom ... [*holding up his homework*]

Elaine: [*With neutral expression on her face, holds up her index finger.*]

Ralph: Mom ... [*becoming impatient*]

Elaine: Ralph, I'm on the phone [*doing her best to keep neutral expression*].

Ralph: You hate me! [*storms out of the room*]

If your child is like Ralph, he may remain upset with you for some time or harbor feelings of resentment. Once your child calms down, it's very important for you to help clarify his understanding of the situation using evidence-based questions, as in the following example.

Elaine: Ralph, did I say that I hate you?

Ralph: [*shakes his head*] Not really ... but *you do.*

Elaine: Why do you think that I'm mad at you?

Ralph: You yelled at me.

Elaine: [*looking surprised*] What did I say?

Ralph: I don't know [*huffing*].

Elaine: I believe I said "I'm on the phone."

Ralph: You were mean ...

Elaine: Because I couldn't get off the phone?

Ralph: [*shrugs shoulders*]

Elaine: Was it my face?

Ralph: [*nods*]

Elaine: What do I always tell you?

Ralph: [*sighs*] It's just your face.

Elaine: Does that mean I'm mad at you?

Ralph: I guess not.

In order to avoid potential misinterpretations, Ralph needs to develop a better understanding of the meaning of facial expressions and gestures. This can be accomplished by following our five-step sequence, drawn in part from the ideas and strategies of Richard Lavoie (2005) and Stephen Nowicki and Marshall Duke (1992):

1. *Tuning in.* Devise two pocket-sized sets of flash cards (one for the parent and one for the child) with the names of general emotional states that your child experiences on a regular basis, such as angry, scared, sad, shy, negative, happy, and tired, among others. For each of these emotions, add at least two other cards showing the names of more subtle shades of that emotion (for example, for angry, you might make cards that say "annoyed" and "agitated"; for scared, you might make cards that read "worried" and "nervous"). On the back of each card include a picture of the facial expression depicting the emotion. Pictures can come from comic books, magazines, family photos, feelings charts, or drawings by any member of the family. Be sure to include your child in this process.

2. *Developing powers of observation.* Using the flash cards, play "guess the emotion" with your child. Taking turns for ten trials, hold up a card and see if your child can identify the emotion shown in the picture. Play every day until your child matches your responses at least 50 percent of the time. Consider giving rewards for meeting this goal. Then continue playing at least once or twice per week until your child matches at least 75 percent of the time. To help your child develop his powers of observation, most notably of facial expressions and gestures, watch family-oriented television shows or movies, or even videos of family events, together with the sound off. Cartoons can be especially useful since body language is often exaggerated. Also, video footage shot at family gatherings like birthday parties can help your child get a second look at expressions during any sibling or peer altercations that might have occurred.

3. *Making sense of social cues.* Act out and guess favorite characters from television shows and movies. To take it a step further, consider mimicking each other in a jocular fashion. If your child is overly sensitive, let family members mimic you first, saying, for instance, "What does Mom look like or do when she gets mad?" What's important here is helping him connect facial expressions and gestures with emotions. (Use your judgment to determine whether or not your child can handle being gently mimicked at first, but work toward helping him tolerate being mimicked, even briefly. Getting your child to laugh at himself will do wonders in toning down his overly serious nature.)

4. *Mastering powers of observation.* Attend family outings at places such as parks, restaurants, or

malls to help your child practice observing others in real-life situations. Prompt him to pay attention to couples, groups of children, and individual peers. Especially relevant scenarios to observe include people having pleasant conversations, others engaged in arguments, kids or adults involved in quiet or aggressive play, and someone being left out. Ask him questions and prompt him to devise stories to explain the circumstances surrounding each situation. Bring along the flash cards and play "guess the emotion" to help him effectively label other people's emotions in natural settings.

5. *Making decisions in context.* As your child becomes more skilled in his powers of observation and his understanding of social cues, help him make good decisions based on his judgments of others. For instance, at restaurants, prompt him to pay attention to your waiter's service. While the waiter is away from the table, help him decide the overall level of service, whether excellent, good, fair, or poor (but do make sure your child understands that this discussion is one that might embarrass the waiter or make his coworkers uncomfortable and so needs to be conducted at a low volume). Next (quietly!) help substantiate his recommendations based on the waiter's manner, promptness, and/or level of courteousness. Do your best to help your child stay focused on the waiter's interpersonal behavior (rather than on the quality of food). Take advantage of feedback cards that some restaurants provide. Similar exercises can consist of evaluating a repair person's level of service (at your home), the quality of a sibling's playdate, or the outcome of a family event.

Understanding voice tone.   Once your child has a better under-standing of facial expressions and gestures, the next step is to help him understand voice tone as an indicator of other people's emotions. For example, to kids who are strong willed like Ralph, any demands such as "Do your homework," "Clean your room," or "Brush your teeth" are more likely to be viewed as an intru-sion and trigger a power struggle. Initially, your demands are made in a low, calm tone of voice. Over time, however, because your child resists cooperating, the tone of your voice naturally becomes louder and more intense. He interprets your voice to mean that you are angry, and so he responds, "You're so mean" or "You hate me." But in fact the tone of your voice has little to do with his interpretation. In fact, if anything, he's probably angry with you but associates your tone with your being angry at him. Essentially, you have to help your child "unlearn" his associations regarding voice tone and pay more attention to the context of situations. Just like Ralph has to learn that a "resting face" (a neutral expression) can indeed be neutral, he needs to understand that voice tone as well is often subtle and unreliable and should be used carefully when interpreting other people's emotions. In the following examples, Elaine helps Ralph let go of his preconceived tonal associations.

1. *Speak softly.* Speak softly and politely when asking your child to do chores. At first, this will be very confusing to him as illustrated below:

Elaine: [*speaking softly*] Ralph, would you please clear the table?

Ralph: [*looks confused*] I'll do it later.

Elaine: [*speaks softly*] Please do it now.

Ralph: [*looks upset*]

Elaine: Am I mad at you?

Ralph: [*shakes his head*]

Elaine: What do I want?

Ralph: For me to clear the table ...

Elaine: Is that okay?

Ralph: [*nods*]

In this example, there is no tone to misinterpret. Ralph has to learn that Elaine is not mad at him simply because she asks him to complete a chore. It's also important to help your child understand the meaning of loud or angry tones of voice.

> 2. *Raise your voice.* Try using a loud voice when asking your child to participate in pleasant events, as illustrated below:

Elaine: [*speaking loudly*] Ralph, do you want to go to the movies?

Ralph: [*smiles*] Yes.

Elaine: Am I mad at you?

Ralph: [*looks surprised*] No ...

Elaine: But I used a loud voice.

Ralph: [*shrugs shoulders*]

Elaine: Does using a loud voice mean I'm angry at you?

Ralph: [*looks confused*] I guess not.

The idea is to practice these exercises until your child no longer automatically assumes that you're angry at him; for instance, he may hesitate for a moment before responding. The next step is to raise your voice a bit when asking him to take on responsibilities. Be sure you ask him "Am I mad at you?" and help him understand that you simply want him to cooperate. (Getting your child to cooperate is another matter, which will be fully addressed in our discussion of Ira and his parents, Horace and Rena, in chapter 8.)

Understanding others' actions. If your child is like Ralph, he may be walking around habitually annoyed, feeling like everyone is mean. This stems in part from his less-developed abilities to read body gestures and voice tone. But he may also be misinterpreting other people's actions, which ultimately causes him to withdraw. Using evidence-based questions, you can help your child make more accurate interpretations of peer-related outcomes, as we illustrate with Ralph and his dad, Len:

Len: Ralph, did you have a good time at the birthday party?

Ralph: [*grimaces*] No ... everyone was mean.

Len: [*looks surprised*] When I got there to pick you up you looked like you were having fun.

Ralph: [*shakes head*] It was the worst party ever.

If the conversation ends here, Ralph will remember that "everyone was mean" and that he had a terrible time at the party. Such an evaluation will strengthen his tendency toward overestimation and make it considerably less likely that he will even attend future parties. The first step is to clear up any misunderstandings.

1. Clarify misinterpretations.

Len: Who was mean to you?

Ralph: [*on the verge of tears*] Everyone.

Len: Which kids?

Ralph: [*shrugs shoulders*]

Len: Can you give me a name?

Ralph: [*hesitates*] Tommy ...

Len: Tommy. Really? He's your best friend.

Ralph: No. Not anymore. I'm never playing with him again.

Len: Did he say anything mean?

Ralph: [*shakes head*]

Len: Did he do anything mean?

Ralph: He wouldn't play with me.

Len: I don't understand. You looked like you were having fun when I picked you up ...

Ralph: [*sighs, looks down*]

Len: You mean when the party started?

Ralph: [*nods head*]

Ralph, like other children with pragmatic learning issues, has overly rigid expectations regarding how his peers *should* behave. And because of his negative filter and difficulty understanding other people's actions, when his peers behave differently than he expects, he takes it very personally. ("Should" statements are also cognitive distortions that have no truth to them. For example, when we say "I should have more money," what we really mean is "I would like to have more money." These statements set us up for disappointment, since they don't have much to do with reality.)

Ralph often feels intentionally excluded from his peers because of incorrect "should" assumptions. Thus, the next step is to help him understand the difference between passive and active peer exclusion. We continue with our dialogue between Ralph and his dad, Len:

2. Explain passive and active peer exclusion.

Len: Was Tommy playing with other kids when you got there?

Ralph: [*nods*]

Len: Did you expect him to just stop playing with them and play with you?

Ralph: [*nods*] He's my best friend.

Len: I know, but if he just left the other kids, how would they feel?

Ralph: Bad.

Len: That's right. Was Tommy really mean to you?

Ralph: [*shrugs shoulders*]

Len: I know you were disappointed that he didn't greet you right away, and you felt left out, but Tommy was just busy with the other kids. Mean is when another kid insults you or refuses to let you play with them. Did that happen?

Ralph: [*shakes head*]

Len: The next time you feel left out, what can you do?

Ralph: Go talk to them.

Len: Sounds good to me. Are you still friends with Tommy?

Ralph: [*weak nod*]

If your child struggles with these issues but also lacks assertiveness, help him practice nonverbal forms of participation and conversational skills as suggested in the discussion regarding Isabelle in chapter 5. Doing so will restore his confidence and help sustain positive social interactions.

Accept responsibility for actions. Because of pragmatic learning challenges and cognitive distortions, Ralph mistakenly felt his peers were excluding him. What he still doesn't understand is how his own behavior negatively affects others. Interestingly, Ralph's peers were rarely mean to him. However, he often alienated them with his sour facial expressions, overly negative remarks, and complaints of aches and pains. If your child has trouble understanding the effects of his own behavior, like Ralph, it's time to help him "see his piece."

Look in the mirror. Ralph, as you know, has a very hard time concealing his emotions. And, since he is habitually annoyed, his sour facial expression (glaring eyes and pursed lips) is always evident. His peers may believe that Ralph is mad at them, but they often have no idea why. Of course, trying to explain this to him proved exasperating. In his mind, nothing was ever his fault. If your child is like Ralph, his thinking style may be very concrete. Thus, subtle hints or suggestions regarding how he's behaving may go over his head. Make your feedback as real and visual as possible.

Elaine helped Ralph become more aware of his sour expression by having him look in the mirror (Nowicki and Duke 1992). As you can imagine, he was resistant to working on his expressions. To make this more acceptable, they both worked on developing friendlier resting faces. In public, Elaine would cue Ralph to change his sour expression by whispering "Face." To help Ralph feel more in control, he was allowed to cue his mother as well by whispering "Smile."

We find videotaping or taking photos of your child's facial expressions in spontaneous social situations to be especially helpful. Showing rather than telling your child that he has an annoyed look (or other unpleasant expression) may prevent a power struggle.

Don't say it. In addition to unfriendly facial expressions, Ralph also needs to curtail his negative talk. We frequently tell our young clients, "You can think anything you want, but you have to be careful about what you say." Help your child become more aware of his negativity by prompting him with "That sounds negative to me." In addition, give him immediate feedback through video- or audiotape. Discuss how he comes across, gently helping him realize that watching or listening to someone else's negativity is unpleasant. The next step is to explain the difference between complaining and more constructive ways of voicing discontent. Emphasize that complaining typically involves a more forceful tone such as anger or disgust, and that it uses emotional words that convey strong dislike, for instance "stinks," "hate," or "horrible."

Express it better. Role-play with your child, taking turns complaining and giving each other feedback. Show him through your nonverbal body language (shaping) that you're not pleased with or interested in hearing his complaints. For instance, minimize eye contact, make uncomfortable facial expressions, or simply walk away. Then, show him how you convey your frustrations in a matter-of-fact way, emphasizing disappointment rather than strong dislike. Continue to practice until your child begins to express his displeasure in more constructive ways, such as saying, "I was disappointed ..." When he does, be sure to give him lots of positive attention.

Once your child's negativity begins to diminish, practice reattribution, like Beverly and Herbert did with George, reframing (saying "Can you say it another way?"), and affirming the positive. This will help him become increasingly constructive and optimistic in his way of thinking and speaking.

Address fatigue. If your child's negativity persists, despite repeated practice of these exercises, it may be time to examine his energy level. For instance, Ralph is fatigued much of the time because of the burden of his pragmatic learning challenges. Given how hard he has to work just to understand the world around him, it's not surprising that he feels irritable, exhausted, and overly negative. On the other hand, George's fatigue was related to his irregular sleep and eating habits, as well as a lack of exercise. Because it can be difficult to know just what's causing fatigue without careful investigation, it's important to examine whether your child's overall well-being and energy level could be improved by any healthy changes to his daily lifestyle.

In Ralph's case, his routine was for the most part adequate. His fatigue was more about his perception of a lack of downtime. He complained of being tired because "I never have any free time." Knowing Ralph, his complaint was likely due to another misperception. In actuality, he had at least two hours of free time after school each day. When Elaine and Len tried to explain this to him, he accused them of being liars. Remember, if your child is like Ralph, because of his concrete way of thinking, explanations often go over his head. To help Ralph understand his schedule, Elaine devised a weekly chart showing Ralph when he had free time. Nevertheless, he remained unconvinced. So, Elaine built in daily periods (thirty minutes each) of free time that would be guaranteed no matter what the circumstances were. Ralph began to feel more secure, and two weeks later he was no longer complaining of feeling tired all the time.

It takes two. If your child is like Ralph, one of your most pressing concerns may be that your child thinks nothing is ever his fault. To help him take responsibility for his part in difficult situations, let's go back to the birthday party. We know Ralph became visibly upset with Tommy. We also know that he mistakenly expected his best friend to greet him immediately upon arrival. What he hasn't revealed, however, is that he yelled at Tommy for failing to greet him. After further probing on the part of his dad, Ralph shared this detail, as the following dialogue illustrates.

Len: Ralph, should we invite Tommy over for dinner?

Ralph: [*shakes head, looks down*]

Len: Why not? You understand why he didn't greet you right away?

Ralph: [*nods weakly*]

Len:	Is there something that you're not telling me?
Ralph:	[*sighs*]
Len:	Ralph ...
Ralph:	I told him, "You're not my friend anymore" [*tone becomes angry*].
Len:	Oh, Ralph ... you yelled at him.
Ralph:	He wouldn't play with me. It's not my fault. I didn't do anything wrong.
Len:	[*taking a deep breath*] I thought we decided that Tommy wasn't being mean.
Ralph:	He was mean.
Len:	Maybe he should have paid more attention to you.
Ralph:	[*nodding*]
Len:	But Ralph, did Tommy deserve to be yelled at?
Ralph:	Not really ...
Len:	I think an apology is in order.

A child like Ralph typically fails to accept responsibility for his actions in one of two ways: he minimizes his part in the interaction and sees only his peer's overreaction, or he justifies his overreaction and sees only his peer's provocation. In order to develop and sustain friendships, he desperately needs to learn about the power of apology. Of course, this is no easy task since he truly sees (and believes) that nothing is ever his fault. In the following example, Len explains how Ralph can apologize and still save face.

Len:	Ralph, let's go apologize to Tommy.
Ralph:	I'm not apologizing to him. I didn't do anything wrong.

Len:	Do you think that when you apologize to someone you're saying, "It's all my fault"?
Ralph:	[nods]
Len:	You're just saying, "I'm sorry that we had a fight." You don't even have to say you're sorry for yelling at him.
Ralph:	Let him apologize first.
Len:	What if he doesn't?
Ralph:	[looks pensive]
Len:	Are you willing to give up his friendship?
Ralph:	[sighs]
Len:	How long have you been friends?
Ralph:	Since kindergarten.
Len:	What do you say? Can you try?
Ralph:	Okay ... but I'm still mad at him.
Len:	That's okay. Apologizing means you still care. We all make mistakes. What will Tommy say when you apologize to him?
Ralph:	That he's sorry too ...
Len:	You bet. And what happens after that?
Ralph:	We're still friends?
Len:	That's right. Are you ready to go apologize?
Ralph:	[smiles weakly]
Len:	Let's go, champ. I'm proud of you.

If your child still refuses to apologize, consider helping him write a brief letter, which can be as simple as the words "I'm sorry."

It's very important that apologizing becomes a family affair. Sometimes, parents believe that because of their greater authority it's inappropriate for them to apologize to a child. They, like Elaine, think that doing so could be perceived as a sign of weakness. On the contrary—apologizing is a sign of strength. If anything, you will be seen as more human and deserving of respect. Do you have friends, relatives, or coworkers who are self-absorbed and appear incapable of apologizing? We all know how frustrating that can be. From dealing with these people, we know that we cannot change the behavior of others, but we can change our own actions, which often changes how others respond to us. This is why apologizing is such a powerful tool.

The time to help your child is now. Remember, his difficulty apologizing is not malicious or personal but rather related to his pragmatic learning challenges and cognitive distortions. But your child will follow your model. Make it your mission to show him the value of apologizing. Doing so will undoubtedly improve the quality of his—and your—peer and family relationships.

Below, we address our next social vulnerability type with our story of Tracey, who, like Ralph, is prone to being neglected by her peers.

Tracey: Becoming Responsible

As you may remember from chapter 3, Tracey is a nine-year-old girl who has difficulty completing tasks independently. At school, Tracey's teachers report that she is easily distracted and has trouble following directions. Her parents, Florence and Scott, are concerned because Tracey is also losing interest in playing sports and seems to be withdrawing from her friends. They wish she would be more focused and motivated and follow through with her responsibilities. Using their social vulnerability checklist for Tracey (see chapter 3), Florence and Scott developed the following goals for Tracey:

Tracey's Organizational Goals

■ Develop better organizational skills

■ Become more self-motivated

As you know, in addition to experiencing social anxiety and social withdrawal, Tracey struggles with some underlying neurological issues (ADD and central auditory processing disorder) that make her socially vulnerable. Because of her withdrawn nature, she is most prone to being neglected by her peers. Tracey ultimately needs to learn how to "tune in" more during her social interactions. In helping her do so, Florence and Scott need to better understand the true nature of Tracey's attentional difficulties, using the following guiding principle: *be mindful of your child's behavior.*

Be Mindful of Your Child's Behavior

Florence and Scott are frustrated by Tracey's lack of responsibility. "I don't understand," remarks Florence. "Tracey's nine years old. She should be able to do her homework or brush her teeth on her own. But if I don't remind her three or four times, nothing gets done. I'm sorry, but I can't accept 'later' as an answer anymore. She can watch television for three hours without flinching but needs to take 'breaks' every ten minutes when doing her homework. Sometimes I wonder if Tracey has a hearing problem. And her room, I can't even go there. What a disaster. After a whole day of Tracey's cleaning, it looks the same, if not worse. I'm really tired. No matter how much I try to help her, she gets mad and wants me to leave her alone. Believe me, I'm tempted to do that. But I can't sit back and watch her fail."

Scott agrees. "It's very difficult to get Tracey to do anything on her own. She's forgetful and loses things. I'm kind of the same way. Flo gets frustrated with me as well and I don't blame her. But I'm getting concerned. Tracey is losing interest in sports and complains of being tired all the time."

On one hand, Florence is right. Tracey should be able to do her homework and take care of herself more independently. But, remember, "should" is a cognitive distortion. What Florence really means is that she would like Tracey to be more independent and responsible. The fact that she's not independent is not Tracey's fault. She is neither lazy nor manipulative. Rather, she struggles with genuine attentional and auditory processing problems. Understanding and accepting that Tracey's behavior is unintentional and reflective of her neurological profile will minimize her parents' feelings of blame and resentment. Nevertheless, constantly reminding and supervising Tracey is not only inconvenient but also exhausting for her parents. There has to be a better way to help Tracey become more independent. Let's see how Florence and Scott go about this.

Develop better organizational skills. The first step is to create a structure that helps the child focus, become more organized, and ultimately successful in fulfilling home and school-based responsibilities. Once Tracey becomes proficient with our six-step sequence, the same process can then be readily applied to social and extracurricular activities.

1. *Identify target areas.* Identify a few key areas in which you would like your child's organizational skills to improve. For instance, Florence and Scott were most interested in helping Tracey become more self-sufficient regarding her homework, chores, and personal hygiene. Be reasonable when selecting these areas for your child, however. Targeting too many areas can easily overwhelm your child and result in minimal or no improvement. In addition, adjust your expectations according to your child's attentional and/or auditory processing issues. This means that expecting your child to automatically take initiative is probably unrealistic and that just providing ample time to complete tasks (without your guidance) is insufficient.

   In addition, you may wish to make some decisions about which tasks are most important. Allowing your child to skip brushing his teeth occasionally is obviously not a good idea. However, does he have to clean his room every day? Florence decided that Tracey's room needed to be organized by the end of the week. She asked Tracey to kindly keep her door closed during the week. And on "clean your room day," Florence helped Tracey with the necessary steps and praised her for being responsible.

2. *Make salient requests and get confirmation.* If your child has attentional or auditory processing issues similar to Tracey's, never assume that he has attended to or processed what you said. For example, Tracey frequently failed to respond to her mother's requests such as "Come for dinner" or "Brush your teeth." Like most parents would, Florence repeated herself three or four times, sometimes going to the point of yelling to get a response. But Florence often called to Tracey from a different room in the house. Instead, it might have helped if she had approached her up close, established good eye contact, and asked Tracey to repeat what Florence had said. In other words, rather than repeating yourself three times, make sure you have your child's full attention the first time. Then, if he fails to respond, you'll know he's not ignoring you. Rather, he is probably hyperfocused on a desired activity, distracted, or confused. Watch for signs that he is confused, such as awkward facial expressions and utterances such as "Huh" or "What?"

3. *Prompt.* Once you have your child's attention and he understands your demands, prompt him to initiate a specific activity. For now, this means escorting him to the bathroom to brush his teeth or to his bedroom to clean his room. Even though you have prompted him and basically gotten him there yourself, praise him for listening ("I like it when you listen") and taking initiative. Of course, if you stop here, he may easily get

distracted and end up doing something else. And if you hover over him, both of you may get frustrated. Instead, help him get started, and develop a suitable monitoring plan.

4. *Help your child get started.* For simple, relatively brief tasks such as brushing teeth, praise your child's progress ("You're doing great!"), and then remove yourself from the situation. When he's finished, compliment him on his responsible behavior. For more complex tasks, such as doing his homework, cleaning his room, or getting dressed in the morning, your initial guidance becomes more important.

   We often take for granted our ability to accomplish the seemingly simple task of cleaning a bedroom. But for a child with attentional and/or auditory processing issues, such a task can be excruciating. First, his room contains an infinite number of distracters such as papers, pencils, books, toys, among other things. Second, what does "clean your room" really mean, anyway? Your child may not know where to begin, and even if he did he might become distracted very quickly and start doing something else. Thus, be specific ("I'd like you to first make your bed"), break down larger tasks into a series of steps, and be prepared to help him get started.

5. *Monitor.* We all hope that taking the time to get your child's attention, prompting, and helping him get started will be enough. And for some socially vulnerable children this will be true. But if your child has attentional and/or auditory processing issues, you will likely need to follow through until completion. This means providing him with periodic "checks" (such as "You're doing great" and "Keep up the good work") to sustain his attention, or additional assistance as needed. In this way, you will help him ultimately be successful. Praise

and emphasize his efforts. Over time, the amount of help you provide your child will indeed diminish. His reliance on your prompts and quick checks, however, may vary.

6. *Practice stimulus control.* Implementing the first five steps will help your child follow through on requests and become more responsible. Now we'd like him to be able to follow through without quite as much involvement from you.

As you know, having to repeatedly tell your child to finish homework or complete chores can quickly become stale—both you and your child can get annoyed after a fairly short time. Hence, any command you deliver repeatedly may come to be perceived as intrusive and result in a power struggle. Using stimulus control will help your child respond more appropriately (without much thought), by learning to associate particular behaviors with specific cues (words, gestures). Once Florence and Scott had Tracey's attention, they cued her with words and gestures. For instance, "Brush your teeth" became "Teeth," accompanied by pointing to her mouth with an index finger. "Do your homework" became pointing to Tracey's backpack. Do your best to make the associations as significant yet gentle as possible. For younger children, you may wish to consider using words and pictures. Practicing stimulus control will make your life a lot easier at home, but, more important, it will also help your child achieve social success.

Tracey's peers had begun to notice her inattentiveness (calling her "Spacey Tracey") and become disenchanted with her careless mistakes during sports activities. To help her combat this problem, Scott practiced a soft-pitched whistle accompanied by a gesture (pointing to his eyes) to get Tracey's attention and cue her to get focused. During games, he helped Tracey sustain her focus by making nonverbal gestures (smiling, clapping, making a "thumbs-up" sign).

Florence helped Tracey practice her conversational skills and worked on nonverbal forms of participation (like Isabelle's parents did in chapter 5) for those times when Tracey had difficulty attending and/or following conversations. For example, Florence worked with Tracey to help her remember to make eye contact, and to use smiles and nods to show her interest in conversations. Once Tracey was using nonverbal communication skills more effectively, Florence taught her to ask questions to keep a conversation going. Doing so helped Tracey remain involved in her peer group instead of calling negative attention to herself by withdrawing.

Develop better motivation.   Our organizational plan can be very effective. But without the proper motivation, it may have limited success. Children with attentional issues often lack internal motivation (Barkley 2005). It's not that they're lazy; it's just part of their neurological profile. Getting upset by your child's lack of responsibility or only giving him extra time to complete tasks doesn't work. If anything, you'll both end up frustrated, and he will likely get punished. This can easily become a vicious cycle, causing undue feelings of resentment. The good news, however, is that over time, with your guidance and support, as well as neurological maturation, your child's internal motivation will ultimately develop. But now, without external motivators, he may idle along at home, at school, and with his peers. How can you provide external motivation?

Consider rewards.   It's important to remember that a reward is not a bribe. A reward is a positive consequence for engaging in a desired behavior. A reward will increase the likelihood of the positive behavior occurring again. With other children discussed in this book, we used rewards to help them overcome shyness or social anxiety as well as take initiative with their peers. If your child is like Tracey, rewards will lead to increased responsibility and independence. There's no need to spend a great deal of money. Instead, your rewards system should consist of the following:

- Small, inexpensive items (for instance, stickers, sports cards, hair accessories)

- Social or home activities (such as renting videos, using television or computer, having playdates)

- Parental praise

Implement rewards. Token programs are useful for encouraging compliance, especially with children who have difficulty waiting. Typically, a predetermined number of tokens (stickers, gold stars, poker chips) are earned for the successful completion of tasks. The tokens are then traded for meaningful tangible, social, or activity rewards. Token programs range from simple sticker charts for younger children to elaborate programs for older children and adolescents (Parker 1999). The latter specifies target behaviors, point values, and points earned on both a daily and weekly basis.

Undoubtedly, these programs can be very effective. However, in some cases, parents and children can come to resent a complicated system. Some parents can get overwhelmed by the effort required to monitor and use such a system, while children can resent the constant reminder of their forgetfulness and ineptitude. We recommend keeping the program simple. It's best to select just a few key target behaviors and be specific about the behavioral expectations needed to earn the contingent rewards. If you'd like, keep track of your child's compliance, but do so in an unobtrusive way. Seeking his involvement in the monitoring process can result in frustration and undue resentment. Instead, periodically (when your child has been particularly successful) show him your chart as evidence of commendable compliance. Doing so now serves as a potent reward, but also as a self-esteem enhancer that will help sustain his motivation. Some general guidelines to consider as you implement your rewards program include the following (Eisen and Schaefer 2005):

- Make rewards contingent upon the successful completion of tasks (with your help, of course).

- Reward as soon as possible after the completion of a task.

- Vary the rewards regularly to prevent "staleness."

- Use the rewards only for the tasks included in the program, not for other tasks, in order to maintain their effectiveness.

- Reward siblings for making progress on their own appropriate goals in order to prevent resentment.

Understand the rewards process.   Parents often ask us, "When do the rewards stop?" In a sense, they never do. Given your child's neurological profile, he may always need some kind of reward to help sustain his attention and motivation. Don't we all? Think of how easy it is to lose interest in an activity that lacks excitement.

In the beginning of the program, small tangible items help to build momentum. Over time, however, take advantage of social and activity rewards that can easily become part of your child's natural environment, such as playing a favorite game with a parent or having a playdate during the week. Also, keep it fun.

Because of Tracey's distractibility, getting ready in the morning was a huge struggle for her, and a frustrating ordeal for her parents. To help Tracey get ready in the morning, the family played a game called the "Race to Get Ready" (Eisen and Engler 2006; Drabman and Creedon 1979). Now, because her parents had turned the morning routine into a game, Tracey viewed getting ready as an exciting challenge.

First, the night before, Florence helped Tracey pack her backpack and lay out her clothes. Second, in the morning Tracey was only permitted two parental prompts to get out of bed. Third, from a distance Florence monitored Tracey's progress as she got dressed, brushed her teeth, and so on. As needed, Florence or Scott gave Tracey cues (such as "Teeth") or provided praise ("You're doing great") to sustain her attention. If Tracey finished her breakfast and was ready to go before the kitchen timer went off, she had won the race. For her reward, she would earn fifteen minutes of doing an activity of her choice with her mom. If she was unsuccessful, Tracey's parents still praised her for her efforts and encouraged her to try harder the next day.

Eventually, in addition to using social and activity rewards, you'll want to help your child use self-rewards. Get him into the habit of saying "I'm proud of myself" for accomplishing his goals. Becoming more efficient and organized, even with your guidance, is the best reward. External motivators will help get him going and sustain his attention. Self-rewards, however, will enhance his self-esteem.

But what happens when your child refuses to comply with your requests? Traditional token programs also include points lost for noncompliance or disruptive behaviors. This adds an element of accountability. The drawback, however, is that at times your child may have a negative balance. When this happens his motivation will greatly diminish and he may lose interest in the program altogether. For this reason, we recommend that rather than losing points and privileges, your child fails to earn the token if he refuses to comply. Nothing is earned and nothing taken away.

Another strategy to consider is using free passes. When her mom asks her to do a particular task, rather than saying "I'll do it later" and never following through, Tracey could ask for a free pass. This means that Tracey is free for one hour. After an hour's time, Florence can prompt her again and Tracey must comply. If she refuses, she loses her free pass for the next day (which can be re-earned for the following day if she complies). Such a strategy will help your child feel more in control and will greatly diminish the likelihood of noncompliance.

On those rare occasions that noncompliance still persists and anger erupts, see chapter 8 for the anger management plan developed for Ira. As a last resort, keep the loss of privileges short and sweet, for instance no television for half an hour.

Remember, children like Tracey have a poor sense of time. Week-long punishments have no greater impact than those that last thirty minutes. In addition, the longer the duration of the consequence, the less likely it is that you will end up being able to enforce it. And if you don't follow through, you weaken your credibility for setting effective future limits. Do your best to create a structure that sustains your child's motivation, helps maintain feelings of control, and most important, paves the way toward increased responsibility and independence.

Get help at school.   As was the case for Ralph, Tracey's deficits are not yet evident in her academic work. This is because their neurological issues (inattentiveness and difficulties with auditory processing; pragmatic learning challenges) are mild, and their superior level of intelligence helps them compensate. At the same time, their parents "carried" them by providing a great deal of home-based support. If your child is like Tracey or Ralph, you know just how much he struggles. You may feel so desperate that at times you might be tempted to step back and let him flounder a bit so his teacher takes notice. But, of course, how could you do that to him? As frustrated as Florence often became, she couldn't let Tracey fail.

As hard as it is to understand, even subtle neurological conditions can negatively affect peer relationships without resulting in poor grades. In fact, it's not uncommon for attention or pragmatic learning deficits to go unnoticed until around middle school. At this time, an adolescent's grades may dramatically slip, which is often misinterpreted as laziness. The reality, however, is that the level of organization required at this age is overwhelming. Your child's compensatory strategies are no longer adequate. If you're concerned about your child's present (and future) academic well-being, do not hesitate to speak to a school counselor about having him evaluated. Become your child's advocate and determine if he is entitled to any remedial services or academic accommodations. Please refer to our supplemental readings at the end of the chapter to help you effectively work through the school's educational support system.

Summary

In this chapter, we have guided you through our step-by-step plans for helping your child or adolescent manage the different forms of social vulnerability most often associated with peer neglect. We discussed strategies to help your child become more tolerant and responsible in both home-based and peer-related situations. In chapter 8, we'll return to Jeremy and Ira and their parents to see how they can learn to better manage the forms of social vulnerability that increase the likelihood of active rejection by peers.

Recommended Resources

Eisen, A., and C. Schaefer. 2005. *Separation Anxiety in Children and Adolescents*. New York: Guilford Press.

Jensen, P. 2004. *Making the System Work for Your Child with ADHD*. New York: Guilford Press.

Lavoie, R. 2005. *It's So Much Work to Be Your Friend*. New York: Simon & Schuster.

Monastra, V. 2005. *Parenting Children with ADHD*. Washington, DC: American Psychological Association.

Nowicki, S., and M. Duke. 1992. *Helping the Child Who Doesn't Fit In*. Atlanta, GA: Peachtree Publishers.

Parker, H. 1999. *The ADD Hyperactivity Workbook for Parents, Teachers, and Kids*. Plantation, FL: Specialty Press.

8

What to Do When Your Child Is Socially Vulnerable and Rejected

I'm getting used to Ira's movements and he's doing a bit better with the other kids. I'm hopeful.

—Horace

Chapter Objectives

In this chapter you will learn the following:

- Guiding principles to help your child become more socially competent

- How to implement a step-by-step program based on your child's unique social needs

- Specific coping strategies for managing the key forms of social vulnerability that are likely to lead to peer rejection

- Anti-bullying tips

When Peer Neglect Becomes Peer Rejection

As you may recall, we have defined social vulnerability as being at risk for being neglected or, even worse, actively rejected by one's peers. But what is the difference between being neglected and being rejected? Children who are neglected by other children are not necessarily disliked, but they tend to be ignored by their peers and may receive few invitations to activities and/or social events. On the other hand, children who are rejected are more likely to be actively disliked, ostracized, and victimized by peers (Bierman 2004). In this chapter, our focus is to guide you through the key forms of social vulnerability that can lead to peer rejection, using the stories of Jeremy and Ira as examples. We begin with Jeremy, who is prone to being both neglected and rejected by his peers, partly due to his inflexibility.

Jeremy: Becoming Flexible

As you may recall from chapter 3, Jeremy is an ambitious twelve-year-old boy who possesses encyclopedic knowledge of maps and landmarks of the United States. He is also a self-proclaimed "Trekkie," and he spends much time alone with his extensive memorabilia collection. At school, Jeremy has difficulty accepting feedback and has an indifferent attitude toward his peers. His parents, Gail and Russell, wish Jeremy could be more flexible, care more about what others think, and make some effort to socialize with his friends. Gail and Russell identified their goals for Jeremy, using his social vulnerability checklist (see chapter 3):

Jeremy's Interpersonal Goals

- Develop empathy

- Become more flexible

Jeremy experiences many of the same social roadblocks that Jessica (lack of social initiative), Beth (social anxiety), and Ralph (misreading social cues) do. For this reason, he can benefit from many of the same strategies utilized with those children. For instance, the cognitive and relaxation-based exercises Beth's parents implemented can help Jeremy manage his social anxiety when speaking on the phone. In addition, like Ralph, Jeremy can practice exercises to learn how to more effectively read other people's body language, especially in situations where he perseverates on topics such as *Star Trek*, and in order to develop a better understanding of how he comes across to others. Gail and Russell can also help Jeremy lighten his indifferent attitude in much the same way as Elaine and Len did with Ralph's negativity. What complicates matters, however, is the fact that Jeremy doesn't seem to care about what others think, which brings us to our next guiding principle, *be mindful of your child's indifference.*

Be Mindful of Your Child's Indifference

Gail and Russell are concerned about Jeremy's lack of interest in being with other people. Gail remarks, "Jeremy doesn't seem to care about what others think, and he rarely gets excited about anything, except maybe his latest Star Trek collectible. We wish he would care more about his appearance. He'll wear the same pair of pants all week, even if they're stained. I guess I should be grateful that Jeremy is not materialistic and superficial, especially since our budget is tight. Even so, I'd give anything if he'd go shopping once in awhile. But what I'm struggling to understand most is that Jeremy does have friends and he seems to like being with them—he just makes no effort."

Russell says, "Jeremy's so rigid and condescending too. I really want us to be close, but he won't let me in. And I'm getting tired of his scornful attitude."

It certainly seems that Jeremy is withdrawn and indifferent to other people. But unlike George (see chapter 6), who withdraws because of social anxiety and depression, Jeremy withdraws as a function of his temperament and neurological profile, which may include features of Asperger's and/or pragmatic learning challenges. In that case, his lack of empathy and his inflexibility may be linked to impaired executive functioning (Ozonoff, Dawson, and McPartland 2002). So it's not that Jeremy doesn't care, but rather that he has difficulty shifting gears (gets stuck) as well as understanding emotions. For Jeremy, remembering facts is easy; understanding subtle and complicated emotions is much more difficult.

Thus, Gail and Russell need to do their best not to take Jeremy's indifference personally. At the same time, to preserve and protect the quality of Jeremy's current and future peer relationships, they will want to play a greater role in helping him initiate social contacts. More important, he needs to learn to compensate by finding comfortable ways to show others that he does indeed care. Let's see how Gail and Russell accomplish their goals for Jeremy.

Develop empathy. Children like Jeremy can learn to show others that they care about them by following our five-step sequence. Once Jeremy masters these skills, he can more regularly take initiative with his peers and forge social connections.

1. *Look at my eyes.* Showing others that we care begins with good eye contact. Nothing conveys our genuine interest in what others have to say more effectively than looking into another person's eyes. And scattered or nonexistent eye contact creates an impression of aloofness and disinterest and is an ultimate turnoff. It may be expected during anxiety-provoking social encounters. But when poor eye contact occurs regularly, however, it's more likely to be a function of a child's neurological profile. Unfortunately, others take it personally and view it as a sign of disrespect—after all, looking at one's conversation partner is such a basic skill that most people do it without thinking.

If your child is like Jeremy, however, looking others in the eye during conversations does not come naturally. For this reason, as a first step, show your child what it's like to be the recipient of poor eye contact. To help Jeremy take notice, Gail and Russell exhibited poor eye contact in an exaggerated form during conversations pertaining to *Star Trek*. If you take a similar approach, keep practicing until your child not only notices your lack of interest but also becomes frustrated. Indirectly, you will be showing (rather than telling) your child the importance of sustaining good eye contact.

Next, during spontaneous conversations, Gail and Russell used shaping to provide Jeremy with minimal attention when he made poor eye contact and lots of attention for making good eye contact. Once Jeremy more regularly demonstrated adequate eye contact, Gail and Russell had him observe their conversations "with his eyes." Afterward, they praised Jeremy's efforts, especially when he showed through his nonverbal body language that he was indeed interested.

To help him learn to apply this skill in a variety of situations beyond the home, be sure to practice stimulus control in real-life situations with friends and relatives. When in public, Gail and Russell would cue Jeremy by whispering "Eyes" and pointing to their own eyes. This was Jeremy's signal to look the target person in the eye or look at some portion of the person's face, such as the nose or forehead. Gail and Russell offered Jeremy plenty of praise for his efforts and small contingent rewards for his willingness to comply. With repeated practice, your child's eye contact will likely improve. But remember, looking at others is still unnatural for her. Thus, at times her need for prompting may be greater than it is at other times, and you may need to continue prompting in unfamiliar or overwhelming situations.

2. *It's not about me.* Like avoiding eye contact, talking too much about ourselves leads others to believe that we're self-absorbed, or even arrogant. Think about what it's like to have a one-sided phone conversation with an overly talkative person. We might be tempted to put the phone down, do a few chores, and pick up the phone again, and we could probably do this without the person's knowledge! For Jeremy, rambling unceasingly about traffic directions or *Star Trek* alienated him from his peers.

So Gail and Russell first helped Jeremy contain his incessant talking about his special interests by establishing "Jeremy time." During these half-hour periods (once or twice a day), Jeremy was free to discuss his special interests while Gail and/or Russell showed enthusiasm. At the same time, Jeremy agreed not to discuss his special interests at home or school outside these intervals. If he slipped at home, Gail and Russell used shaping to redirect his conversations. They did this by praising him for catching himself talking about *Star Trek* and for switching to a subject of greater interest to others, and for any attempts to start or continue conversations about topics of interest to others. In public, they practiced stimulus control by whispering "Enough" or making an agreed-upon gesture with their hands to mean "Time." For good compliance, they dispensed small contingent rewards.

The second part of the program was intended to help Jeremy become more familiar with relevant peer-related topics, sports, and current events, and help him to get more comfortable discussing them with other kids. Gail and Russell role-played with Jeremy, shaped his behavior with their nonverbal body language, and developed a series of generic questions that he could ask his peers. Then, when he didn't know what to say, he could ask his peers questions to keep conversations going. Gail and Russell also helped him develop focused questions and statements about specific topics, once a generic question had gotten the conversation back on track. For those times when he became socially anxious, his parents helped him practice observing other kids' interactions with his eyes. To help him become less self-absorbed, during dinner family members were required to ask each other three questions about their day, modeling appropriate interest in each other's experiences and ideas.

3. *Look sharp.* Unfortunately, no matter how well Jeremy shows an interest in other kids, if his personal hygiene and dress code are below par, his peers won't give him a second look. Worse, he'll stand out. When Jeremy forgets to shower, doesn't comb his hair, or wears the same pants every day, he tells others that he doesn't care about himself. Hence, how could he possibly care about anyone else? To Jeremy, however, physical attractiveness was unimportant—he thought that what really mattered was science and science fiction. Gail didn't disagree about the unimportance of attractiveness, but she tried hard to help Jeremy understand that his peers valued clothes and looking sharp. If Jeremy wanted to fit in, he needed to make some effort to conform.

    Gail was tired of her constant power struggles with Jeremy over this issue and decided she would leave it up to Russell to take him clothes shopping. This turned out to be a good idea and, in fact, helped improve Jeremy's relationship with his dad. As a family, they decided that if Jeremy took better care of himself on weekdays, he could relax his efforts over the weekend.

4. *Manage special interests.* With repeated practice of the previous steps, Jeremy was beginning to present himself in a more favorable way. However, he claimed that he had "no time" to socialize. And he was right, but only

because he was spending an inordinate amount of time developing Web sites, collecting road maps, and building *Star Trek* models. As a result, Gail and Russell decided to set some limits on his access to these activities. At the same time, however, they made greater access contingent upon his willingness to take social initiative with his peers. At first, Jeremy was angry and most resistant to this idea. He ultimately agreed to try as long as he could earn a chance to get additional *Star Trek* memorabilia.

5. *Take social initiative and participate in activities.* The next step is to implement a program similar to the one Ann and Ron used with Jessica (see chapter 6), which allows your child to take initiative with her peers but still feel in control. You'll want to emphasize your child's efforts and consider contingent rewards as necessary. With his parents' encouragement, Jeremy began taking initiative with friends and good acquaintances (communicating in phone calls, e-mail, and chats at school). However, Jeremy's efforts were obligatory and a function of his strong sense of fairness, which made him feel responsible for following through with the program. In addition, Gail and Russell were not completely satisfied, and they wanted Jeremy to participate in at least one after-school activity. After lengthy discussion and brainstorming, Jeremy relented and decided to volunteer at the local animal shelter. If you'd like your child to participate in an activity to help promote his empathy, perspective taking, and social development, consider the following possibilities:

   ■ Work with animals (Stewart 2002). Animals tend to be more accepting than peers and can help children develop a better understanding of nonverbal signals. As part of Jeremy's program, he worked toward adopting a puppy based on his efforts to initiate social contacts and sustain a better attitude with his family and peers.

- Enroll in acting or arts programs. Acting and arts facilitate perspective taking (pretending to be others), empathy, and creative self-expression (rather than anger).

- Facilitate teaching opportunities. If your child needs to feel in control and competent, she may relish telling others how to do things, especially when it comes to her special interests. Set up weekly meetings where she can educate family members on useful topics that they wish to learn about (rather than being perceived as bossy, eccentric, or annoying).

- If you suspect your child might be gifted, look into gifted-child programs. Your child might find activities that interest her and enjoy opportunities to interact with like-minded peers. (See chapter 9 for a discussion of giftedness and social vulnerability.)

Become more flexible. Children with a combination of anxiety and neurological issues are often chronically inflexible and prone to explosive outbursts. Because of biological and neurological sensitivities, your child may be frequently overwhelmed and hence continually feel out of control. The resulting rigidity and inflexibility is her desperate way of sustaining control. In other words, she cannot tolerate much change. In Jeremy's case, chronic inflexibility created problems for him at home, at school, and with his peers. For instance, because of his refusal to accept feedback, and in view of his intelligence and academic performance, his teachers learned it was easier to simply appease him. At home, as much as Gail and Russell wanted to be involved with Jeremy's schoolwork, the power struggles and explosive outbursts became too much to handle, so they too left him alone. Jeremy's inflexibility, however, took on dangerous dimensions during car trips.

With Jeremy's encyclopedic knowledge of road maps and landmarks, he was insistent that his parents abide by his directions. When she was driving, Gail reluctantly acquiesced. Russell, on the other hand, felt that as Jeremy's parent and the driver of the car, he was entitled to make his own decisions. As you can imagine, Jeremy did not respond well, often kicking the car seat and screaming obscenities. On more than one occasion an accident almost resulted. Gail and Russell were forced to limit Jeremy's travel to trips that were absolutely necessary. Jeremy was clearly in dire need of learning to become more flexible, so Gail and Russell implemented our four-step sequence to promote enhanced flexibility.

1. *Identify target areas.* First, identify a few key areas where your child needs to demonstrate improvement. Gail and Russell were most interested in facilitating Jeremy's flexibility regarding homework and school-related projects, car trips, and shopping at stores. Once again, be reasonable and realistic. Remember that your child's inflexibility is probably long-standing and the product of her anxiety and neurological sensitivities. Initially, help her take small steps and emphasize her efforts.

2. *Educate about and reward flexibility.* Explain what it means to be flexible, for example doing something the other person's way when you would very much like to do it your way. Then devise flexibility coupons or tickets (you can create them on the computer or purchase a roll of carnival tickets) and keep them in your pocket, purse, or wallet. You can use them to help your child become flexible in a variety of situations, such as doing homework, completing chores, and accepting another family member's way of doing things. On the back of the coupon, write what your child's reward will be. Of course, like tokens, these coupons can be collected and traded for bigger rewards. Be sure your child understands that you get to decide whether she is being flexible. If your child continues to be resistant to the

teacher's feedback, help her see that she can show others that she is agreeable by compromising and considering the feedback, even if she doesn't initially agree. Doing so will help preserve and improve the quality of her relationships.

3. *Practice in real-life situations.* Once your child gets into the habit of being more flexible, you can attempt to have her try some more challenging situations. For Gail and Russell, this meant car trips and shopping at stores. In order to give Jeremy opportunities to practice being flexible, Gail and Russell implemented some short, low-pressure car trips. They expected him to want to give directions, but his parents hoped he would be motivated enough to try to earn a coupon. Because there was no time pressure to get somewhere, Gail and Russell were at their relaxed and patient best. Jeremy responded favorably to the short trips, but longer excursions proved more challenging. For this reason, Gail and Russell compromised and let Jeremy dictate directions for specified portions of the trip, but they decreased these periods in duration and frequency over time.

Now that Jeremy was able to be more flexible, a similar plan needed to be developed for shopping trips, since Jeremy wanted to dictate where to shop and what to buy. Any arguments often fueled public explosions. For this reason, the family first visited one store for a single item, and then worked toward larger shopping lists. As long as Jeremy earned coupons for flexibility, Gail and Russell continued to compromise. To round out the plan, Jeremy was required to cooperate with his teacher and both parents at least one time per day. The nature of the task being asked of him and whether he followed through were not deemed crucial. Rather, his willingness to be flexible with a respectful attitude was emphasized. Over time, Jeremy was expected to do more cooperating with adults than refusing.

4. *Practice flexibility in peer-related situations.* Each of the
    children discussed in this book struggles with inflex-
    ibility, which hurts their peer relationships. Because of
    their anxiety and neurological issues, they feel a need to
    be in control, are overly possessive, and often insist that
    other children do things their way. You undoubtedly
    want your child to be able to loosen up and become
    flexible with other children, in order to improve her
    relationships. You want her to be able to say okay to
    another child's way of doing things. Initially, you may
    need to supervise some of your child's social situations
    and encourage her to be flexible by offering coupons
    during the interactions. Eventually, promising ahead
    of time that you will give your child a coupon if she
    practices flexibility during a playdate will be a sufficient
    motivator. It won't take long before your child's peers
    respond positively to her newly developed agreeable atti-
    tude. (We have found that using coupons in these situa-
    tions works more effectively than using tokens, probably
    because the child decides spontaneously, within reason,
    what each coupon will be worth at the time of receiv-
    ing it. Flexibility coupons are also effective ways to help
    children "unlock" in anger-provoking scenarios.)

Let's now look at our final social vulnerability type, as shown in
Ira's story. Unlike Ralph, Tracey, and even Jeremy, Ira is more prone
to being actively rejected by his peers because of the intrusive nature
of his struggles.

Ira: Becoming Respectful

As you may recall from chapter 3, Ira is an energetic ten-year-old
boy who moves around constantly and has frequent meltdowns. At
school, Ira constantly calls attention to himself. The other kids see
him as different and annoying and bully him every chance they get.
His teacher simply thinks that he is immature. His parents, Horace

and Rena, are overwhelmed. They wish Ira could learn to "keep to himself" a bit more and become more respectful toward others. After completing the social vulnerability checklist (see chapter 3), Horace and Rena outlined the following goals for Ira:

Ira's Self-Control Goals

- Develop better self-restraint

- Respond more effectively to bullying

Like Ralph, Ira struggles with some underlying neurological issues (ADHD, sensory processing problems) that make him socially vulnerable. But Ira's issues make it more likely that he will actively interact with his peers (generally inappropriately so), hence there is a greater likelihood that he will be actively rejected. Ira ultimately needs to learn how to tone down his interactions with others. But at the same time, Horace and Rena need to better understand the nature of Ira's movement needs, and they can do this by following our next guiding principle, *be mindful of your child's needs for activity and affection.*

Be Mindful of Your Child's Activity and Affection Needs

"There is never a dull moment in our house," says Horace. "Ira is always doing something, like careening up and down the stairs, practicing karate in the living room, tapping the dinner table, singing, or shrieking. He seems like a happy kid so full of energy, and I'm glad. I wish he could just play quietly sometimes. Ira's always begging me to roughhouse with him, but, honestly, I'm afraid I'll get hurt. Ira gets overstimulated so quickly that once he gets started he loses control. Maybe it's asking too much, but it would be nice once in a while, especially after work, to have some peace. I'm not always up to dealing with him."

"Ira has meltdowns without warning, and if I ask him to do anything he says he hates me," agrees Rena. "I know he doesn't mean it, but I can't help resenting him. I'm exhausted and I never have any time for myself. I cannot leave Ira alone with David, our four-year-old son, even for a minute. Ira is sweet and affectionate but squeezes the life out of him. And I'm afraid to answer the phone, since Ira is always getting into trouble at school. He says the other kids bully him. I want to help him but I don't know what to believe. His stories change like the weather. I wish Ira could learn to handle himself better [with his peers]."

Horace and Rena understand why Ira is rejected by his peers. He's impulsive, rough, and loud, and he has frequent meltdowns. But he doesn't act this way on purpose. Because of sensory processing issues, Ira craves constant stimulation through his bodily movements and "annoying" behaviors. He literally needs to be doing something constantly. At the same time, he is extremely sensitive to being touched. This is why he has trouble telling the difference between an accidental bumping in the hall and an intentional act of bullying. And, because of his impulsivity, he has minimal ability to stop and think about the logical consequences of his behavior. If your child is like Ira, it's important to accept his high activity and affection needs as long as they remain at tolerable levels.

Remember, his constant need to move around is not something that he can control. Although his behaviors may be difficult for you to handle, regularly showing Ira through nonverbal body language or telling him that he is being annoying will only contribute to his already low self-esteem, which has been lowered further due to bullying. If anything, children like Ira need to feel overwhelmingly accepted at home. Of course, this is no easy task given their overly demanding nature and behaviors. Let's see how Horace and Rena accomplish their goals for Ira.

Develop better self-control. A major problem for Ira is that he loses control too easily, usually becoming belligerent or having an explosive outburst, and this behavior occurs at home, at school, and during social or extracurricular activities. It's becoming increasingly evident that sensory processing problems are often associated with anger, rage, and explosive outbursts (Cheng and Boggett-Carsjens 2005). Just like Ralph becomes easily fatigued from the burden of his pragmatic learning challenges and withdraws, Ira explodes because of constant sensory overload. Ira's ability to cope with sensory input is influenced by a variety of factors and can easily fluctuate from day to day or even over a period of hours. For this reason, Horace and Rena implemented our five-step sequence that includes both sensory and anger management strategies (Biel and Peske 2005).

1. *Identify sensory sensitive areas.* The first step is to identify your child's undersensitive areas (those in which he craves stimulation) and oversensitive areas (those where he cannot tolerate stimulation). Ira was undersensitive to touch and activity. This is why he craved "deep touch" and constant stimulation in the form of incessant, frenzied movement and expression. At the same time, he was oversensitive to certain tastes, loud noises, and bright lights. As a result, he avoided or became easily overwhelmed when confronted with particular foods, noises, and brightly lit places such as cafeterias.

2. *Satisfy sensory needs (undersensitive areas).* Horace and Rena helped satisfy (and channel appropriately) Ira's need for deep touch by giving him nightly baths and back rubs as well as weekly swim lessons. In addition, Horace agreed to roughhouse with Ira twice a week for brief intervals with clear ground rules. Horace praised Ira for keeping himself under control and, if he was successful both times, rewarded him with an additional wrestling session. The family gave hugs as rewards for Ira's efforts to calm down and be more respectful.

   At school, Ira used a stress ball when necessary. To help satisfy Ira's frenzied need for movement and expression, the family scheduled game nights twice a week. These activities, such as charades and telling jokes, were unrestricted and without a lot of rules. The idea was to give Ira ample opportunities to be silly, loud, and excited. If Ira behaved relatively appropriately (considering the unruly nature of the games), keeping his hands to himself and taking turns, for example, his parents rewarded him with another game over the weekend. If you take this approach with your child, you'll want to keep in mind that success is the most important thing here. If she gets completely overstimulated, keep the games brief, set clear ground rules, and provide plenty of praise.

3. *Monitor oversensitive areas.* Given Ira's oversensitivity to loud noises and bright lights, Horace and Rena did their best to monitor, and restrict if necessary, Ira's exposure to places such as malls, cafeterias, and concerts. In addition, when appropriate, they provided Ira with earplugs and/or noise-canceling headphones for listening to music. Horace and Rena were also careful not to overschedule Ira, keeping his calendar free of too many extracurricular activities, in order to lessen his load of general sensory information. In addition, like Elaine and Len did for Ralph, Horace and Rena scheduled daily downtime for Ira.

   Helping your child develop good habits will also enable her to better manage overwhelming sensory input. For Ira, Horace and Rena ensured that he got adequate sleep and they did their best to encourage a balanced diet. Adequate nutrition, especially sufficient protein, is extremely important for children like Ira (Monastra 2005; Biel and Peske 2005). Of course, given Ira's taste sensitivity, he was extremely resistant to eating foods other than macaroni and cheese, pizza, and plain bagels, so it was a challenge to get him to eat a variety of nutritious foods.

   Do your best to introduce new foods to your "picky eater" without applying undue pressure. Help her be open to trying small amounts, with the goal of adding one or two healthy foods to her repertoire every week. Consider offering contingent rewards (that are not food related), and give plenty of praise for her efforts to try rather than emphasizing that she eat any specific amounts.

4. *Practice stimulus control.* Implementing the first three steps will help your child stay in balance on a more regular basis, and as a result she will experience fewer unpredictable and intense outbursts. However, she still needs to learn self-restraint in social situations, and this is a tall order. Understanding to use an "inside voice" in the car, for instance, is one thing; remaining quiet for any length of time is another. Parents of kids with sensory processing issues and/or impulsivity, like Ira, often feel like a broken record. Telling them to be quiet is of no use. What they need is stimulus control—an approach to teaching behavior that involves helping your child respond more appropriately (without much thought) to certain situations by associating particular behaviors with those situations.

The first step is to create appropriate situations for your child to meet her sensory needs. For instance, with repeated practice, Ira began to associate family game play, roughhousing with his dad, and swimming with acceptable times to be active and silly. Thus, he was more likely to contain himself in other situations.

The next step is to help your child associate key situations with the need to contain herself. For instance, Horace and Rena took turns taking Ira to the library and their house of worship during less crowded hours, as well as on short car trips. As Ira became antsy and noisy, they would prompt him to be quiet by using a gesture and would praise him for following through. With practice, Ira learned to remember to ask "Where am I?" and then answer ("library," or "house of worship"), which helped him quiet down. When you try this strategy with your child, start out by keeping the situations brief, low pressure, and geared toward helping your child be successful. Use plenty of praise and consider, if necessary, using small contingent rewards.

After a while, you can try other situations that require quiet and calm behavior.

To teach Ira to keep his hands to himself, Horace and Rena also cued him by saying "Hands" and making a gesture (hands up, then down to the side). First, they practiced this when Ira played with his younger brother, David. When he had gotten the hang of responding to the cues, they arranged short supervised playdates with close friends and relatives, followed by regular activities such as karate.

It's important to remember that your child's behavior is *context specific*. This means that your child's social restraint in one situation is not likely to generalize to other even similar situations, and this can be very confusing for parents if they don't realize what's going on. For instance, Rena became upset with Ira for acting inappropriately at a family gathering when he had done so well at a similar gathering the week before. The difference was that the first gathering was at their house, and she prompted and praised him regularly. The second gathering, however, was at a relative's house, and Rena permitted Ira to socialize on his own. So keep your expectations realistic to avoid undue feelings of resentment and frustration, and state your expectations for your child whenever you're entering an unpracticed situation.

5. *Manage anger.* The ability to respond to anger appropriately goes a long way toward building self-esteem, facilitating learning, and improving social relationships for a child like Ira. As a first step, help your child practice deep breathing and muscle relaxation exercises as illustrated in Isabelle's story (chapter 5). You can also use shaping by giving her maximum positive attention for her efforts to calm down and minimal attention for acting out. Be sure to validate her feelings by saying

something like "I know you're upset but I cannot talk to you until you're calm." Then do your best to ignore her angry behavior as long as it remains at tolerable levels, and offer your help once she has calmed down.

6. *Tame explosive outbursts.* You may find that your child's explosive outbursts can be intense and seemingly unceasing at times. When this happens, you may want to help her "unlock" by providing small tangible or activity-based rewards for remaining calm for a speci-fied period of time. Use your judgment here, taking into account the intensity of the outburst and your child's age. We usually recommend one to five minutes, and we advise starting with a shorter time period and gradually increasing to longer times.

This reward strategy can be very effective. However, some parents, understandably, cannot help but resent their child's outbursts and find it difficult to dispense rewards under these circumstances. In that case, what typically happens is that the outburst goes on indefinitely, and, as a matter of survival, the parent may give in to the child's demands. Unfortunately, doing so encourages both the frequency and the intensity of the outbursts. Our reward strategy short-circuits your child's outbursts and rewards her ability to calm down under extreme circumstances. This is what you want, and ultimately, over time, her outbursts will be shorter and less intense.

Sometimes a child's outbursts may include spe-cific problem behaviors, such as Ira's screaming "I hate you" at his parents. This was something that Rena could not accept. Of course, we're not condoning disrespect and it needs to be addressed. But your child is prob-ably not exactly rational at the height of the explosion. Because of sensory overload and impulsivity, Ira was literally out of control. What he really meant to say was "I'm so mad at you!" Do your best to minimize your personal response to your child's remarks, and keep in mind what she really means. We recommend that you prompt her as the outburst is coming on or afterward, when she's calm again, to self-correct, by asking her, "Are you sure that you want to say that?" If she says something more appropriate or "takes it back," praise her efforts and discount her tirade. Then discuss your hurt feelings and encourage an apology. If she refuses to self-correct, consider a small, potent consequence such as removal of a privilege (such as one television show or computer session). If self-correcting is ineffective, and your child is very hard on herself ("I'm an idiot" or "I hate myself"), consider giving her an occasional and much-needed "do-over." Help her understand that everyone makes mistakes and you understand that self-control is hard for her. You can reinforce that if she keeps trying to calm down she is entitled to a second chance. After much practice and rewards for calming down, Ira began to self-correct and "catch himself" before exploding.

In addition to teaching the skill of self-correcting, we also recommend using "chill-outs" rather than time-outs. Besides sensory overload, anxiety, and impulsivity, loss of personal control is another reason why children explode. A time-out (for instance, being told "Go to your room") can feel like a loss of control since it is often executed with strong emotional overtones. And to kids without an accurate sense of time, even short specified time intervals can be overwhelming.

During chill-outs, however, your child is in charge. You are merely suggesting that she appears angry and it would be a good idea for her to try to calm down (in her room or other place) before it's too late. Make it clear that she can decide when her chill-out is over. Consider using contingent rewards if necessary and praise her for using chill-outs willingly. Chill-outs are consistent with stimulus control. You are telling your child that it's okay to get angry (everyone does), but that she needs to do so in an appropriate place.

If the child refuses to comply, she would not earn the contingent reward. If she continues her outburst, first validate her feeling (for instance, saying "I know you're upset"), and then shape her behavior ("I will talk to you when you are calm"). As we recommended earlier, rather than focus on the length of the outburst, praise your child for any ability to calm down. Discuss a reward for her willingness to take a chill-out the next time.

Of course, chill-outs work best at the beginning of the outburst, if clear signs of agitation are present. But as you know, your child's outbursts can often occur without warning, so it can be difficult to catch the behavior before it goes too far. For this reason, role-play when your child is calm, and discuss (after the storm) using chill-outs as a strategy for the next time.

7. *Respect your child's time frame.* Another way to help your child feel in control is to respect her time frame for managing her emotions. For example, Rena is a "now" person. She doesn't like being angry at family or friends, and she wants to solve problems immediately. Ira, however, is a "later" person. Given his sensory issues and impulsivity, he needs time to process emotions before discussing difficult situations. Confronting him too quickly or forcefully may result in his lying and/or exploding. When he lies or loses control, he's telling his parents that he's overwhelmed and cannot think clearly. Thus, whatever thoughts pop into his head may get expressed. If his parents continue to force a discussion at that time, his fabrications or his out-of-control behavior will escalate.

For this reason, give your child ample time to settle down. We recommend giving one or two "free passes" per day. A free pass means that you will leave her alone (not force a discussion) for a short period of time (up to thirty minutes) so that she can reflect and figure out how to best approach you.

Free passes and chill-outs can be used as individual strategies in your toolbox for handling a variety of situations. Free passes are used in situations where you need to discuss an event with your child—for example, something that she's done wrong that she is likely to lie about. The child can continue doing what she was doing for a short period of time, but she is required to participate in the discussion at the end of the time period. On the other hand, a chill-out is used in a situation of conflict—for example, when your child has become frustrated with her homework and doesn't want to continue. A chill-out involves validating the child's feeling (frustration, upset) and asking her to willingly remove herself from the situation so she can express her anger in a more appropriate way. So both strategies can be effective, depending on the situation.

8. *Put it all together.* At the same time, work to create a family environment where everyone can say what they feel without worrying about repercussions. Consider an open family forum like the one Beverly and Herbert implemented with George (see chapter 6).

As you help your child become more socially skilled, find her new social opportunities (such as sports, clubs, hobby groups) with groups of kids she doesn't already know. This way she can start fresh and have increasingly positive experiences. This is true for all children who are socially vulnerable. More important, you also need to become charter members of your child's fan club. Of course, with her struggles, this can be no easy task. But a family climate of acceptance and understanding will go a long way toward helping your child manage not only her anger but also the emotional overload from being bullied.

Respond more effectively to bullying.   Your most pressing concern may be to help your child deal with being bullied by her peers. Given his "in your face" nature, Ira is highly vulnerable to being seriously rejected. With repeated practice of the previous exercises, Ira will now show better social restraint with his peers. But Ira is still not prepared to deal with verbal bullying. He needs some anti-bullying tips:

> *Anti-bullying strategies.*   A number of approaches have been recommended for addressing bullying (Freedman 2002; Lavoie 2005; Nowicki and Duke 1992). These include passive, neutral, and assertive strategies.
>
> Passive strategies include *ignoring* and *self-talk*. With these strategies, your child learns to remain calm during a confrontation and to minimize the attention that she gives the bully and his henchmen. Ignoring makes sense, since bullies naturally pick on children who cannot defend themselves or who make these confrontations into public spectacles. In practice, however, it may not always work for a child like Ira, because even when Ira does ignore insults from his peers by refraining from speaking or walking away, he cannot hide his body language, which clearly shows his distress (he might grimace, pout, or be on the verge of tears). Thus, in actuality, he is not really ignoring. More typically, a child like Ira will shut down, cry, or become hostile. For this reason, consider more empowering strategies such as self-talk.
>
> Self-talk is the use of coping thoughts to stay calm during a bullying or other stressful confrontation. For example, your child could silently say to herself, "Relax," "Stay calm," or "Take a deep breath." But after repeated practice and much role-playing, Ira still "forgot" to say these words when he had run-ins at school or the playground. This was indeed frustrating for Rena and Horace. To make this approach more effective, they decided to cue Ira with gestures like they had done when teaching him to keep his hands to himself and to remain quiet ("Hands" and "Quiet"). This time, however, gestures consisted of pointing to the nose ("Breathe in through the nose") and slowly moving a hand downward ("Stay calm"). They cued Ira during strained interactions with his peers at birthday parties and karate

instruction. To increase the likelihood of generalization at school, Rena and Horace enlisted the support of Ira's teacher. Although she wasn't always aware of the more-subtle bullying incidents, she helped Ira cope with his frustrations.

We find that neutral strategies such as *agreeing* or *complimenting* (Freedman 2002; Lavoie 2005) can be helpful with children like Ira and Ralph. The idea behind these strategies is to stun the bully, or throw him "off balance." Bullies expect strong reactions from their victims. Imagine the bully's response if Ira said, "You're right, I'm stupid." If anything, the bully would now be upset and, after a while, would grow tired of bullying Ira. Given Ira's oversensitivity, however, it would be very hurtful for him to say such a thing. He would likely take it to heart and feel bad about himself. We prefer complimenting the bully by saying the opposite of his derogatory remark. Role-play, pretending to be a bully, and help your child respond as follows:

Bully: You're stupid.

Child: Not everyone is as smart as you.

Bully: You have no friends.

Child: Not everyone is as popular as you.

Bully: You're such a klutz.

Child: Not everyone is as athletic as you.

Keep practicing and role-playing until your child's responses become automatic. This way, she doesn't have to think about comebacks. You can also quietly cue her by whispering "Opposite."

Both Ira and Ralph had great difficulty understanding the difference between playful ribbing and mean-spirited teasing, especially sarcasm. If this is true for your child, help her use humor as another neutral strategy to defuse bullying confrontations. Humor, like agreeing and complimenting, is not the reaction bullies are looking for, and it's a wonderful and simple strategy: if you don't know what to say or do, just laugh.

You and your partner can teach your child about sarcasm and teasing by ribbing each other until she is laughing hysterically. Then you can invite her to tease you in appropriate but not overly silly ways. The next step is to role-play situations in which your child is being teased, and coach her to respond with laughter.

Continue practicing until your child cannot help but burst with laughter. Praise your child's sense of humor and give her a high five. To promote generalization, practice in real-life settings such as parties, family gatherings, and extracurricular activities. Expect her to become upset when others are sarcastic, but help her use humor to defuse the situation. Use contingent or spontaneous rewards as needed to help her "unlock" and get refocused.

It should also be kept in mind that the effectiveness of any anti-bullying technique depends on a child's ability to anticipate the context of bullying situations. And since the context is always changing, and your child's ability to anticipate may be limited, there is always the possibility that it could backfire. We recommend simple but bold tactics that can be implemented and practiced to the point of becoming automatic, and that can be used when the other techniques don't seem to be working. For instance, help your child respond to harassing remarks or physical acts by saying "Stop it!" "Leave me alone!" or "I don't like it when you do that."

Perhaps the most important anti-bullying strategy is to seek out help in an effective way. Ira too frequently responded impulsively with anger and shouted the names of the culprits. Doing so certainly did not endear him to his peers, who branded him as a "tattletale." Make sure that your child understands and accepts the difference between reporting harmful behavior and being a tattletale. Role-play until your child responds correctly with "Don't tell" or "Get help" as you spontaneously throw out concrete examples. Practice in real-life social settings, and secure the support of her teacher at school.

Getting support. The next step is to empower your child by developing a comprehensive system of support, over time, that includes peers, teacher(s), coaches, mental health professionals (school psychologist, social worker, or guidance counselor), and administrators. Do your best to develop a relationship with your child's teacher through phone calls or e-mail without being intrusive. Seek regular updates, and demonstrate appreciation for the assistance, even if he or she is largely unresponsive. Be tactful if you need to move up the school's hierarchy, taking care not to undermine anyone's authority. More often than not, the school psychologist or social worker can become an important source of support.

Inquire about anti-bullying programs, school-wide character education, or friendship clubs. If unavailable, offer to get involved and consider distributing anti-bullying materials. Talk with other parents and gently inquire about their children's peer-related issues. Harness their support, especially if bullying is occurring in the school. It's not uncommon for administrators to minimize (or even deny) the extent of bullying in their school, unless, of course, several parents come forward to ask that changes be made.

Make connections in your community through your local parent-teacher organizations. Some school districts have special education organizations (SEPTA), which are especially helpful in bringing together like-minded parents who can provide each other with understanding, support, and guidance as they muddle through the complexities of the school system. These parents, like you, have children who grapple with anxiety, learning disorders, and related neurological problems and are too frequently misunderstood and bullied, and they can help you feel less alone in your struggles.

Summary

In this chapter, we've guided you through our step-by-step plans for helping your child manage social vulnerability associated with peer rejection and bullying. We discussed strategies for helping your child become more flexible and respectful in both home-based and peer-related situations. And we set the stage for the development of healthier family and peer relationships. In chapter 9, we'll help you evaluate your child's progress and determine whether seeking professional help would be beneficial.

Recommended Resources

Beane, A. 1999. *The Bully Free Classroom*. Minneapolis, MN: Free Spirit Publishing.

Biel, L., and N. Peske. 2005. *Raising a Sensory Smart Child*. New York: Penguin Books.

Freedman, J. 2002. *Easing the Teasing*. New York: McGraw-Hill.

Greene, Ross W. 2005. *The Explosive Child*. New York: Harper Paperbacks.

Jensen, P. 2004. *Making the System Work for Your Child with ADHD*. New York: Guilford Press.

Lavoie, R. 2005. *It's So Much Work to Be Your Friend*. New York: Simon & Schuster.

Lockshin, S., J. Gillis, and R. Romanczyk. 2005. *Helping Your Child with Autism Spectrum Disorder*. Oakland, CA: New Harbinger Publications.

Monastra, V. 2005. *Parenting Children with ADHD*. Washington, DC: American Psychological Association.

Nowicki, S., and M. Duke. 1992. *Helping the Child Who Doesn't Fit In*. Atlanta, GA: Peachtree Publishers.

Olweus, D. 1993. *Bullying at School*. Malden, MA: Blackwell Publishing.

Parker, H. 1999. *The ADD Hyperactivity Workbook for Parents, Teachers, and Kids*. Plantation, FL: Specialty Press.

Sprague, J., and H. Walker. 2005. *Safe and Healthy Schools*. New York: Guilford Press.

9

Taking the Next Step

I'm beginning to think that Tracey's distractibility is beyond her control.

—Florence

Chapter Objectives

In this chapter you will learn the following:

- How to make sense of your child's progress

- Some benefits of working with a mental health and/or medical professional

- The importance of taking care of your own needs

Making Sense of Your Child's Progress

When you are evaluating your child's progress, it's important to take into account the complexity of his social struggles. For instance, relatively self-contained problems such as shyness, social anxiety, and mild forms of social withdrawal generally respond effectively to treatment, and they also lend themselves to clearer, more observable outcomes. In this case, you can readily see your child's improvements regarding his degree of phobic avoidance, social initiative with peers, and participation in social and extracurricular activities.

In many cases, like with Isabelle (slow to warm up), Stephen (self-conscious), Beth (anxious around performance situations), and Jessica (socially withdrawn), phobic avoidance can be largely minimized, and socialization with peers greatly improved. Of course, it's important to remember that your child's slow-to-warm-up nature or tendency toward social anxiety still remains. This is why social exposures need to be ongoing and become an integral part of his life.

However, you may be dealing with challenges that are far more complex, and your child's progress may be inconsistent and at times unclear. This is due to possible neurological conditions (such as ADD/ADHD, sensory processing issues, or pragmatic learning challenges), anxiety, and accompanying personality characteristics such as chronic inflexibility. As a result, helping him may be an ongoing process that requires longer-term efforts.

The Severity of Your Child's Problems

In addition to considering the complexity of your child's social struggles, it's important to take into account how much his difficulties are interfering with his family, peer, and academic functioning. For example, Paul's social phobia was pervasive, George's social withdrawal led to depressive symptoms, Ira's victimization by peers was chronic, and Jeremy was becoming a compulsive hoarder (Chansky 2000; Fitzgibbons and Pedrick 2003).

Under these circumstances, children often need comprehensive therapist-assisted programs that can address social anxiety and related problems. The strategies in this book may help your child feel more in control, enhance his self-esteem, and ultimately improve the quality of his family and peer relationships, but it's best to view our program as a first step. If you haven't already done so, we encourage you to seek out a qualified mental health professional, especially if your child's struggles have spilled over into his schoolwork and are affecting his academic functioning. When anxiety and related problems exert a broader and more intense influence, children and adolescents become increasingly vulnerable to experiencing clinical forms of depression and/or suicidal behavior.

Suicidal Behavior

Approximately 3 million youth exhibit suicidal behavior or attempt suicide each year (Naparstek 2006). Although it is uncommon in children under twelve years of age, suicide is the third leading cause of death for youth aged fifteen to nineteen. Risk factors for suicidal behavior include the following associated problems (Evans et al. 2005):

- Behavioral difficulties (depression, drug/alcohol abuse, impulsivity, anxiety)

- Family history and patterns (suicidal behavior in other family members, lack of cohesion, lack of support)

- Environmental factors (negative life events, significant loss, peer victimization)

When they occur together, these risk factors may contribute to feelings of hopelessness. Unlike helplessness, which is often temporary, hopelessness is the feeling that nothing will ever improve. Hopelessness has been shown to be an important predictor of suicide (Rotheram-Borus and Trautman 1988). Previous suicidal behavior, not surprisingly, is the strongest predictor of future suicidal behavior (Hawton and Sinclair 2003).

Thus, depression and suicidal behavior are major concerns for our youth. Because of the triple threat (the interactions among temperament, anxiety sensitivity, and neurological conditions; see chapter 3), socially vulnerable children and adolescents are at risk for having strong emotional reactions such as explosive outbursts, chronic fatigue, overwhelming anxiety, and depressive symptoms. As these reactions persist, become increasingly pervasive, and are accompanied by ongoing family and environmental stressors, socially vulnerable children may have an increased likelihood of experiencing depressive disorders and suicidal behavior. Some signs that your child may be considering suicide include the following (Barnard 2003; Naparstek 2006):

- Dramatic changes in behavior (mood, energy, appetite, sleep)

- Increased risk taking

- Comments about death or dying

- References to others who have committed suicide

- Giving away valued possessions

- Themes of death in child's music, art, essays, or poems

- Availability of firearms or toxic pills

- Recent and devastating loss (death of family member, or breakup of a relationship)

Your child may make comments about death or dying sporadically in the context of overwhelming frustration ("I wish I were dead") or during a period of sad and withdrawn behavior. The latter is more alarming, but any comments about suicide, even if your child is referring to a friend's behavior, must be taken seriously. Be alert for signs that your child feels worthless and/or hopeless (for example, if he is a victim of chronic bullying) and also makes reference to suicidal behavior. If you suspect that your child is experiencing symptoms of depression and/or considering suicidal behavior, it is crucial that you contact your family pediatrician, school counselor, or qualified mental health professional. In the event of an emergency, call one of the hotlines listed at the end of this chapter.

What About Bipolar Depression?

Up to this point in the book, we've been emphasizing social vulnerability stemming from a combination of temperament, anxiety sensitivity, and neurological conditions. But children and adolescents may become socially vulnerable for other reasons, most notably bipolar depression. Bipolar depression is a mood disorder in which youth experience both depressive and "manic" episodes, often alternating rapidly (for instance, within hours or days). Depressive symptoms include feelings of sadness, tearfulness, a lack of interest in pleasant events, as well as appetite and sleep disturbances (see chapter 2). Manic episodes in adults are characterized by elevated or expansive mood (for instance, feeling overly powerful, confident, and invincible), boundless energy (minimal need for sleep), pressured speech, risk-taking behaviors (such as shopping sprees or compulsive gambling), poor judgment (impulsivity), and hypersexuality (marked interest in sexual materials; greater risk for extramarital affairs) (American Psychiatric Association 2000).

Diagnosing youth with bipolar depression is extremely controversial for several reasons. First, it's difficult to distinguish normal "moodiness" and behavioral problems from genuine mood disorders. Second, children may not experience mania as adults do.

For example, mania in children is often expressed in the form of extreme irritability—a symptom that is not unique to bipolar depression and is associated with a variety of behavioral problems. Thus, it remains questionable whether childhood symptoms are truly reflective of mania.

Children with bipolar depression are not only socially vulnerable, because of their extreme emotionality, prolonged outbursts (lasting several hours), and impulsivity, but they are also at risk for gang and/or cult involvement, accidents, suicidal behavior, self-injurious behavior (cutting, for instance), substance abuse, and criminal activities (Waltz 2000). Bipolar depression is a serious and potentially incapacitating disorder, and, if left untreated, it can have long-term ramifications for children and their families. Early intervention is crucial. If you feel that your child may be experiencing signs of bipolar disorder, consult with a child and adolescent psychiatrist specializing in mood and related disorders promptly.

A Word About Giftedness

Several of the children depicted in this book have characteristics of giftedness, which may also result in social vulnerability in youth. Widely accepted definitions of "giftedness" include general intellectual or specific abilities (for instance, math, science, or music) in the upper 3 to 5 percent of the population (Webb et al. 2005) and/or IQ scores of 130 to 155 (Karnes and Johnson 1986). IQ scores above 165 constitute profound giftedness (seen in prodigies, for instance).

It's not surprising that some gifted youth have trouble fitting in with peers, given their intellectual advancement, quirkiness, and unique interests. Gifted youth may experience uneven development referred to as "asynchrony," in which, for instance, intellectual skills develop more rapidly than physical and/or emotional ones. This leaves the child or adolescent feeling out of balance socially and emotionally (Silverman 1995, 2000). To complicate matters, gifted youth may experience other problems as well, including attentional, sensory, relational, and/or learning disorders. These "twice exceptional" children are at great risk for becoming socially vulnerable. Their learning challenges may remain undetected due to compensation involving their considerable intellectual strengths. If your child is experiencing social, emotional, and/or behavioral issues and displays significant intellectual strengths, do not hesitate to have him evaluated. Early intervention addressing any special academic or unique social needs can make all the difference in his school-related and social adjustment.

The Benefits of Professional Help for Your Child

Let's face it: when it comes to helping our own children, being objective is no easy task.

We're too close to the situation. Sometimes, the guidance of an unbiased third party can be a powerful resource in our struggle to help a child overcome shyness, manage social anxiety and withdrawal, or build peer relationships. Professional guidance can help sustain your child's progress.

Is the process of helping your child one big power struggle? Remember, if your child is socially vulnerable, he may regularly feel fatigued, overwhelmed, or out of control. Asking him to do anything, at times, may literally be too much for him, and it may provoke an explosive outburst or further social withdrawal. Of course, if he possesses a strong-willed temperament, he will be even less likely to comply with your requests.

Too many power struggles or failed attempts to change a child's behavior can leave any parent feeling overwhelmed, resentful, and exhausted. And you certainly can't always be up for handling his social, emotional, and peer-related struggles, especially if you don't have adequate family support (for example, if you're a single parent, or your spouse or partner is not involved in childrearing). A qualified therapist will establish realistic treatment goals as well as set effective limits with your child or adolescent. You will no longer be perceived as bad or mean since the therapist now becomes responsible for structuring the program. Over time, as your child becomes increasingly independent, flexible, and cooperative, the therapist will help you set effective limits on your own and support you in doing so.

Another benefit of working with a qualified therapist is that he or she will incorporate periodic follow-ups into the program. These visits can be used to refresh out-of-practice coping skills or to stimulate problem-solving skills in anticipation of stressful transitions.

Considering Medication

In our experience, most children and adolescents with mild to moderate social anxiety and/or withdrawal respond favorably to therapy and are not candidates for medication. As psychologists, we believe in the power of cognitive behavioral therapy (CBT) and other evidence-based psychological treatments. But we also understand that many childhood problems are influenced by biological, neurological, and emotional sensitivities.

Sometimes, even the guidance of a qualified mental health professional is not enough to deal with these sensitivities, and so at some point you may need to consider medication as part of your child's treatment regimen. Medication is typically considered only when social anxiety and/or withdrawal are chronic enough to result in widespread phobic avoidance and/or lead to unremitting depressive symptoms. Medication clearly has value for children struggling with these sensitivities, and at times it may be instrumental in helping a child or adolescent begin the process of overcoming anxiety and related problems. Medication in combination with CBT may also help in crisis situations where severe anxiety (for instance, OCD, panic, or school refusal), depression, or suicidal behavior has emerged, effectively reducing the crisis so psychological treatments can be utilized.

More typically, however, medication may be needed to help your child more effectively regulate his feelings. He may not be in crisis, but perhaps he frequently becomes overwhelmed with emotion (for instance, explosive outbursts), or his constant negativity may have reached intolerable levels. He is showing you that the continuous strain of his social vulnerability is too much. If this happens, your family's relationships are also likely to be completely disrupted (for instance, parent-child, marital/partner, and/or sibling relationships), and treating your child with medication may help restore a sense of balance in your family. Finally, medication may assist your child to more effectively manage the academic and/or behavioral issues that stem from having a specific neurological disorder (such as ADD/ADHD).

If your child or adolescent's circumstances do lead you to consider medication, we recommend working with a psychiatrist who specializes in treating anxiety and related problems in children and adolescents. Such an individual can carefully monitor your child's response to medication as well as any side effects experienced. Your child's pediatrician can probably help you find a qualified professional.

Taking Care of Your Own Needs

Most parents who complete our program have worked hard to help their children with their social struggles. During the process, however, they don't always make the same investment of time and energy in their own well-being.

Taking care of your family should be of central importance. However, effective parenting most often results when parents also take care of their own needs, especially when their child or adolescent has ongoing social, emotional, and/or behavioral issues. Raising children with such issues is extremely stressful, exhausting, and sometimes discouraging. That's why respite and pleasant activities are so important for caregivers, in addition to being essential components of a healthy family process. If you've been reluctant or simply haven't had time to pursue your own interests, socialize with friends, or go to the gym, it's time to take steps toward a more active, self-nurturing lifestyle. Both you and your family will benefit.

Taking Care of Your Own Mental Health

Nurturing one's own needs and seeking professional help for a child are important steps, but they may not always result in effective solutions. Sometimes, a parent may also need professional help to take care of his or her own mental health needs.

Trying to manage the social, emotional, behavioral, and academic needs of your socially vulnerable child alone can be overwhelming. What about the rest of your family's needs? What about sustaining some sense of order in your house? What about keeping up with your work responsibilities? If you haven't been able to do it all, you may feel like a failure as a parent, spouse, or partner. After all, you feel like you should be able to handle everything. (Remember, "should" is a distortion. What you really mean is that you would like to be able to handle your situation better.) But under these circumstances, handling everything on your own may not be realistic, and trying to do so may make you vulnerable to anxiety, depression, or physical problems.

Chronic fatigue, worry, and/or social withdrawal can limit any parent's ability to help their child. Stress resulting from other sources such as family conflict, marital issues, or a lack of emotional or financial support can also interfere with a parent's ability to help his or her child. If you feel you could benefit from professional help, consider contacting your internist or local mental health center for referrals. Remember, you are an indispensable member of your family and someone your loved ones depend on and cherish. Because of this, you must take care of your own needs and mental health. Make it a priority.

Summary

Whether you have followed the lessons of our program on your own or worked with the assistance of a qualified mental health and/or medical professional, you've taken important steps to help your child overcome shyness, manage social anxiety and/or social withdrawal, and, most important, helped to improve and protect his social well-being.

Recommended Resources

800-SUICIDE

800-THERAPIST

References

Albano, A. M., and M. F. Detweiler. 2001. The developmental and clinical impact of social anxiety and social phobia in children and adolescents. In *From Social Anxiety to Social Phobia: Multiple Perspectives*, edited by S. G. Hofmann and P. M. DiBartolo. Needham Heights, MA: Allyn and Bacon.

American Psychiatric Association. 2000. *Diagnostic and Statistical Manual of Mental Disorders*. 4th ed., text revision. Washington, DC: American Psychiatric Association.

Asher, S., and J. Parker. 1989. Significance of peer relationship problems in childhood. In *Social Competence in Developmental Perspective*, edited by B. Schneider, G. Attili, J. Nadel, and R. Weissberg. Dordrecht: Kluwer.

Barkley, R. A. 2005. *Attention-Deficit Hyperactivity Disorder: A Handbook for Diagnosis, Assessment and Treatment*. New York: Guilford Press.

Barlow, D. H. 2002. *Anxiety and Its Disorders: The Nature and Treatment of Anxiety and Panic*. 2nd ed. New York: Guilford Press.

Barnard, M. U. 2003. *Helping Your Depressed Child: A Step-by-Step Guide for Parents*. Oakland, CA: New Harbinger Publications.

Beck, J. S. 1995. *Cognitive Therapy: Basics and Beyond*. New York: Guilford Press.

Biel, L., and N. Peske. 2005. *Raising a Sensory Smart Child: The Definitive Handbook for Helping Your Child with Sensory Integration Issues.* New York: Penguin Books.

Bierman, K. L. 2004. *Peer Rejection: Developmental Processes and Intervention Strategies.* New York: Guilford Press.

Chansky, T. E. 2000. *Freeing Your Child from Obsessive-Compulsive Disorder.* New York: Three Rivers Press.

Cheng, M., and J. Boggett-Carsjens. 2005. Consider sensory processing disorders in the explosive child: Case report and review. *Canadian Child and Adolescent Psychiatry Review* 14:44–48.

Coloroso, B. 2003. *The Bully, the Bullied, and the Bystander.* New York: Harper Resource.

Dawson, P., and R. Guare. 2004. *Executive Skills in Children and Adolescents: A Practical Guide to Assessment and Intervention.* New York: Guilford Press.

Drabman, R. S., and D. L. Creedon. 1979. Beat the buzzer. *Child Behavior Therapy* 1:295–96.

Eisen, A. R., and L. B. Engler. 2006. *Helping Your Child Overcome Separation Anxiety or School Refusal: A Step-by-Step Guide for Parents.* Oakland, CA: New Harbinger Publications.

Eisen, A. R., and C. E. Schaefer. 2005. *Separation Anxiety in Children and Adolescents: An Individualized Approach to Assessment and Treatment.* New York: Guilford Press.

Evans, D. L., E. B. Foa, R. E. Gur, H. Hendin, C. P. O'Brien, M. E. P. Seligman, and B. T. Walsh. 2005. *Treating and Preventing Adolescent Mental Health Disorders.* New York: Oxford.

Fitzgibbons, L., and C. Pedrick. 2003. *Helping Your Child with OCD: A Workbook for Parents of Children with Obsessive-Compulsive Disorder.* Oakland, CA: New Harbinger Publications.

Freedman, J. S. 2002. *Easing the Teasing: Helping Your Child Cope with Name-Calling, Ridicule, and Verbal Bullying.* New York: Contemporary Books.

Friedberg, R. D., and J. M. McClure. 2002. *Clinical Practice of Cognitive Therapy with Children and Adolescents: The Nuts and Bolts*. New York: Guilford Press.

Goodyer, I. M., and P. Cooper. 1993. A community study of adolescent depression in girls: The clinical features of identified disorder. *British Journal of Psychiatry* 163:374–80.

Hamaguchi, P. A. 2001. *Childhood Speech, Language, and Listening Problems: What Every Parent Should Know*. New York: John Wiley & Sons.

Hartup, W. W. 1992. Friendships and their developmental significance. In *Childhood Social Development: Contemporary Perspectives*, edited by H. McGurk. Hove, England: Erlbaum.

Hawton, K., and J. Sinclair. 2003. The challenge of evaluating the effectiveness of treatments for deliberate self-harm. *Psychological Medicine* 33:955–58.

Kagan, J., J. S. Reznick, and N. Snidman. 1986. Biological bases of childhood shyness. *Science* 240:167–71.

Karnes, M. B., and L. J. Johnson. 1986. Identification and assessment of gifted/talented handicapped and non-handicapped children in early childhood. *Journal of Children in Contemporary Society* 18(3–4):35–54.

Kearney, C. A. 2005. *Social Anxiety and Social Phobia in Youth: Characteristics, Assessment, and Psychological Treatment*. New York: Springer.

Kendall, P. C. 1992. Healthy thinking. *Behavior Therapy* 23:1–11.

Kendall, P. C., and J. P. MacDonald. 1993. Cognition in the psychopathology of youth and implications for treatment. In *Psychopathology and Cognition,* edited by K. S. Dobson and P. C. Kendall. San Diego, CA: Academic Press.

Lavoie, R. 2005. *It's So Much Work to Be Your Friend: Helping the Child with Learning Disabilities Find Social Success*. New York: Simon & Schuster.

Lockshin, S. B., J. M. Gillis, and R. G. Romanczyk. 2005. *Helping Your Child with Autism Spectrum Disorder: A Step-by-Step Workbook for Families*. Oakland, CA: New Harbinger Publications.

Monastra, V. J. 2005. *Parenting Children with ADHD: 10 Lessons That Medicine Cannot Teach*. Washington, DC: American Psychological Association.

Nansel, T. R., M. Overpeck, R. S. Pilla, W. J. Ruan, F. Simons-Morton, and P. C. Scheidt. 2001. Bullying behaviors among U.S. youth: Prevalence and association with psycho-social adjustment. *Journal of the American Medical Association* 285:2094–2100.

Naparstek, N. 2006. *Is Your Child Depressed? Answers to Your Toughest Questions*. New York: McGraw-Hill.

Nowicki, S., and M. P. Duke. 1992. *Helping the Child Who Doesn't Fit In*. Atlanta, GA: Peachtree Publishers.

Ollendick, T. H., and J. A. Cerny. 1981. *Clinical Behavior Therapy with Children*. New York: Kluwer/Plenum Press.

Olweus, D. 1993. *Bullying at School*. Malden, MA: Blackwell Publishing.

———. 1995. Bullying at school: Knowledge base and an effective intervention program. *Annals of the New York Academy of Sciences* 794:265.

Olweus, D., S. Limber, and S. Mihalic. 2000. *Blueprints for Violence Prevention, Book Nine: Bullying Prevention Program*. Boulder, CO: Blueprints for Violence Prevention Series.

Ozonoff, S., G. Dawson, and J. McPartland. 2002. *A Parent's Guide to Asperger Syndrome and High Functioning Autism: How to Meet the Challenges and Help Your Child Thrive*. New York: Guilford Press.

Parker, H. C. 1999. *The ADD Hyperactivity Workbook for Parents, Teachers, and Kids*. Plantation, FL: Specialty Press.

Patterson, G. R. 1982. *Coercive Family Processes*. Eugene, OR: Castilia Press.

Rotheram-Borus, M. J., and P. D. Trautman. 1988. Hopelessness, depression and suicidal intent among adolescent suicide attempters. *Journal of the American Academy of Child and Adolescent Psychiatry* 27:700–704.

Seligman, M. E. P., K. Reivich, L. Jaycox, and J. Gillham. 1995. *The Optimistic Child*. Boston, MA: Houghton Mifflin.

Silverman, L. K. 1995. The universal experience of being out-of-sync. In *Advanced Development: A Collection of Works on Giftedness in Adults*, edited by L. K. Silverman. Denver: Institute for the Study of Advanced Development.

———. 2000. The two-edged sword of compensation: How the gifted cope with learning disabilities. In *Uniquely Gifted: Identifying and Meeting the Needs of the Twice Exceptional Student*, edited by K. Kay. Gilsum, NH: Avocus Publishing.

Smith, S. G., and J. R. Sprague. 2003. The mean kid: An overview of bully/victim problems and research based solutions for schools. *Oregon School Study Council Bulletin* 44:2.

Sprague, J. R., and H. M. Walker. 2005. *Safe and Healthy Schools: Practical Prevention Strategies*. New York: Guilford Press.

Stewart, K. 2002. *Helping a Child with Nonverbal Learning Disorder or Asperger's Syndrome*. Oakland, CA: New Harbinger Publications.

Strauss, C. C., and C. G. Last. 1993. Social and simple phobias in children. *Journal of Anxiety Disorders* 7:141–52.

Tanguay, P. B. 2001. *Nonverbal Learning Disabilities at Home: A Parent's Guide*. London: Jessica Kingsley Publishers.

Walker, H. M., E. Ramsey, and F. M. Gresham. 2004. *Antisocial Behavior in School: Evidence-Based Practices*. Belmont, CA: Wadsworth.

Waltz, M. 2000. *Bipolar Disorders: A Guide to Helping Children and Adolescents*. Sebastopol, CA: O'Reilly and Associates.

Webb, J. T., E. R. Amend, N. E. Webb, J. Goerss, P. Beljan, and F. R. Olenchak. 2005. *Misdiagnosis and Dual Diagnoses of Gifted Children and Adults: ADHD, Bipolar, OCD, Asperger's, Depression, and Other Disorders*. Scottsdale, AZ: Great Potential Press.

Andrew R. Eisen, Ph.D., is associate professor in the School of Psychology and director of the Child Anxiety Disorders Clinic at Fairleigh Dickinson University. His research and clinical interests include child anxiety and related problems, learning disorders, and sensory integration issues. Eisen has published numerous journal articles and book chapters as well as seven books including *Helping Your Child Overcome Separation Anxiety or School Refusal*, *Separation Anxiety in Children and Adolescents*, and *Clinical Handbook of Childhood Behavior Problems*. He maintains a private practice focusing on children and families at the Center for Neurofeedback and Integrative Health (www.cnih.net) in Bergen County, NJ.

Linda B. Engler, Ph.D., is codirector of the Child Anxiety and Related Disorders Clinic in Bergen County, NJ. Her research and clinical interests include child anxiety and related problems, ADHD, and the early detection and remediation of nonverbal and language-based learning disorders. Engler has published and presented in the areas of anxiety disorders, ADHD, eating disorders and school partnerships. She is coauthor of *Helping your Child Overcome Separation Anxiety or School Refusal*.

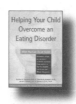
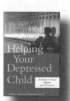